**THE**
**THINKING PERSON'S**
# GUIDE TO
# SOBRIETY

# THE
# THINKING PERSON'S
# GUIDE TO
# SOBRIETY

## BERT PLUYMEN

ST. MARTIN'S PRESS ❧ NEW YORK

Library of Congress Cataloging-in-Publication Data

Pluymen, Bert.
    The thinking person's guide to sobriety / Bert Pluymen.
       p.     cm.
    Originally published: Austin, Tex.: Bright Books, © 1996.
    Includes bibliographical references.
    ISBN 0-312-20034-X
    1. Alcoholics—Rehabilitation.   2. Alcoholism—Treatment.
   3. Recovering alcoholics.   4. Alcoholics Anonymous.
   I. Title.
   HV5276.P58   1999
   362.292'86—dc21                   98-43649
                                                CIP

ISBN 0-312-20034-X

First published in the United States by Bright Books

First Edition: March 1999

10 9 8 7 6 5 4 3 2 1

*For Paula and Harry, my mom and dad*
*and my wonderful sister, Anita*
*with all my love*

# CONTENTS

◨

## PART ONE: WAKE-UP CALL

**CHAPTER FIVE**

## PART TWO: RECOVERY

**CHAPTER SIX**

**CHAPTER SEVEN**

**CHAPTER EIGHT**

**CHAPTER NINE**

**CHAPTER TEN**

## PART THREE: PERSONAL & SCIENTIFIC SNAPSHOTS

**CHAPTER ELEVEN**

**CHAPTER TWELVE**

**CHAPTER THIRTEEN**

## CHAPTER FOURTEEN

## CHAPTER FIFTEEN

## CHAPTER SIXTEEN

## CHAPTER SEVENTEEN

## CHAPTER EIGHTEEN

## CHAPTER NINETEEN

## CHAPTER TWENTY

## CHAPTER TWENTY-ONE

# ACKNOWLEDGMENTS

I owe a debt of gratitude to many people for their encouragement and assistance. To Professor John Trimble, author of *Writing with Style: Conversations on the Art of Writing,* for his expert literary advice and invaluable editing, not to mention his unwavering faith in the book. To David H. Smith of DHS Literary, Inc., who I am proud to call my agent. To Jennifer Enderlin, my enthusiastic editor at St. Martin's Press. To Dr. Carl Erickson, head of the Addiction Science Research and Education Center, University of Texas at Austin. To Glenda Hathaway for her dedicated transcriptions. To Melinda Longtain, Ph.D., for her magnificent guidance, and to Frank Ivy, Neal Carson, Cecilia Hunt, Enrique Toro, Gypsy Cole, Shay St. John, Dona Seitsinger, and Ray Chester for their support. To the remarkable men and women who freely shared the most intimate details of their lives so that their experiences might assist others. And, finally, to all the scientists and researchers who have dedicated their careers to finding a solution to this vexatious puzzle.

# AUTHOR'S NOTE

W hen I quit drinking eight years ago, my family, friends, and law partners all said: "You don't have a drinking problem. Why are you stopping?" But they didn't wake up in my body on a Saturday when I'd feel horrible. I once heard that orange juice was good for a hangover, so I'd drink half-a-gallon with aspirin. Then I'd look in the mirror and promise myself that I'd never, *ever* do that again. And I wouldn't. For about three weeks.

I would also stop drinking completely for a week, a month, even three months. Then I'd think, *I don't have a problem with alcohol. I can stop anytime I want.* So I'd say, "Give me a beer. Please! . . . In fact, make that two." I had no idea that alcohol addiction was an off-and-on disorder and that half of all addicted people are not drinking in any given month.

When I got sober I had a severe case of the "yets": I had yet to be arrested, yet to lose a job, and no drinking in the morning or shaking hands for me, thank you. But I knew that alcohol was a problem because I was regularly trying to moderate how much I drank. And the desire to drink moderately is known only to guess who? People with drinking problems. Normal men and women drink moderately without giving it a second thought.

And even though my drinking didn't interfere with work, my personal life was in a shambles, which prompted my recovery, as well as the chapter entitled, "Thirty Minutes of Begging Is Not Foreplay."

Luckily I met many people in sobriety with drinking stories similar to mine. I could see myself in their lives, and perhaps you will, too. Included here are the eloquent voices of women (a marathoner, British flight attendant, basketball star, chemical engineer, and interior designer) as well as men (a writer, Australian entrepreneur, realtor, and San Francisco investor).

How do women and men of good will become addicted to alcohol?

Well, we know that addiction runs in families and that some people are genetically predisposed to the disorder. In fact, I have one friend who laments, "If I hadn't inherited my alcoholism, my family would have left me nothing."

However, for every person like him, with an unfortunate genetic tendency toward addiction, there are two of us who apparently manage to acquire this disorder on our very own. How? Through years of heavy social drinking. And what influences us most is the culture in which we live.

I once saw a bumper sticker that said, "God Created Alcohol So the Irish Wouldn't Conquer the World," and later realized that was an accurate reflection of the impact culture has on our drinking behavior. Many Irish men raise pint after pint with a group of their mates at the pub because that is integral to their culture. And in this country, if you closed your eyes while speaking to some people in their thirties and forties, you'd think you were talking to a nineteen-year-old. They still call each other during the week to plan Happy Hour on Friday, a lake party on Saturday, and a beer-and-chips football gathering on Sunday. As a result, they *normalize* each other's drinking behavior.

And the greatest difficulty is that it's not the elbow that becomes addicted, but the brain. The very organ that likes alcohol is trying to determine whether to change the behavior. Guess what it will always decide? That's why *The Thinking Person's Guide to Sobriety* advises, "Your Mind Is Like a Bad Neighborhood: Never Go in There by Yourself."

Many women today drink like the guys, not realizing that their bodies are more sensitive to alcohol. And when they become more intoxicated, some naturally blame their smaller size. But if you selected a woman and man of equal weight, say 125 pounds, and gave them both the same amount to drink, do you know who would be more intoxicated? The woman. Do you know by how much? Her blood-alcohol level peaks *40 percent* higher than the guy's. That has terrible implications, not only for her behavior, but women averaging just two drinks a day have a significantly higher risk of contracting invasive breast cancer.

We forget that alcohol is a toxin so harmful that one of every three addicted people dies of a heart attack. Half die of either heart disease or cancer. Average age of death: fifty-two. By contrast, liver disease kills only 2 percent. Because I like irony, I'll read the newspaper when a prominent person dies of a heart attack at age forty-five to see if the family says, "Joe just loved life," or friends remark, "Jane lived life to its fullest."

Many of us have poisoned ourselves striving to have fun. And don't get me wrong: *I still want to have a good time.* After I'd been sober a year, I promised my support group that if life was not as much fun sober, I would go back to drinking. But when one of my old drinking buddies later offered to take me to "retox," I declined because life was good—and promising to get better. Through the lives of sober friends, I could see dreams becoming reality.

In fact, if you are performing at 80 percent of your capacity and life is going fairly well, but your dreams are unfulfilled, why not function at 100 percent and have your fondest dreams in life come true?

One of my dreams was to stop practicing law, and I could never figure out how to do that while I was drinking. Now my greatest fear if I ever start drinking again isn't that I'll end up on a sidewalk or in jail, but in a law office; and the secretary will come in and say, "Mr. Pluymen, your next client is in the waiting room." I'll think, *Damn, when did I start drinking again?*

Bert Pluymen

To contact the author, write:
P.O. Box 9802-306
Austin, Texas 78766
E-mail: BPluymen@aol.com

# THE
# THINKING PERSON'S
# GUIDE TO
# SOBRIETY

# PART ONE

# WAKE-UP CALL

# 1

## BOTTOM'S UP!

M y name is Bert . . . and, uh, I have a desire to stop drinking."
The difficult words came haltingly out of my mouth. Around
the room sat total strangers, except for the one good friend whom
I'd asked to bring me. The strangers smiled sympathetically. I
choked back tears that would soon overwhelm me in this unknown
place.

My friends would never have fathomed my being here. I was a
trial lawyer who had twice been recognized in *The Best Lawyers in
America* on the recommendation of judges and fellow attorneys.
Earlier, I had been named the outstanding young lawyer in Austin,
Texas. I had argued and won a major case in the United States
Supreme Court just two years out of law school. I had been
cocounsel in the three-month jury trial over the Howard Hughes
estate that eventually resulted in a $50 million payment to the
State of Texas.

I had never been arrested for drunk driving, public intoxication,
or anything else. I'd never hit another car because of drinking.
Never had a memory loss due to drinking. Never had complaints
from friends, law partners, women I dated, or anyone else about
my drinking—or even about any single occasion when I drank.

So what on earth possessed me to ask my friend to take me to a
meeting of anonymous people who had chosen not to drink
anymore? It was because my wife of six months had just left me to
spend her life with another man—and I *knew* that I would die if I
drank enough to stop the incredible pain.

Excruciating as that experience was, it unwittingly presented
me with an opportunity to have a high bottom, a good place to get

off the descending elevator of alcohol. "Fifth floor? . . . Thanks, I'll get off here." No sense in riding this baby to the third floor of the basement.

At the time, all I knew was that I faced a clear choice. I could either stay sober, and walk through my pain of rejection and abandonment one day at a time, or I could drown the feelings in alcohol . . . and die.

Staying sober had the advantage of getting to the other side as quickly as possible, but offered no relief from the agony. Drinking offered the allure of temporary pain relief, but risked death because of the amount of alcohol required to mask the feelings. Even if I survived the attempt to anesthetize my feelings, I would be dealing with painful hangovers while wallowing in self-pity and prolonging the recovery process indefinitely.

What made me think that I was capable of reacting to tragedy by drinking so much alcohol that I could die? To answer that, I have to tell you my story.

## The Fun's Just Beginning

My discovery of alcohol did not begin at home. Neither Mom nor Pop drank, unless you consider a glass of sherry during the holidays "drinking." There was no obvious genetic predisposition to my affection for the fruit of the vine.

I had been born in Holland and spoke no English when my coal-miner family immigrated to America. I was just ten. School in Holland had always been easy for me, and my first semester in America, I made all As except for a B in English. Of course, I was your typically driven immigrant child, a product of parents who gave up all they had to move four thousand miles to a foreign place, with no job or family or friends in sight.

I was a curiosity piece in my Port Arthur, Texas, grammar school because of my heritage and accent. Being a celebrity was fun, but it was also dangerous—boys would pick fights with me because I was different, the dappled horse in the chestnut herd. Teachers liked me, though, because I was courteous and made good grades. Most students accepted me, too. By high school, I was president of

the student body, quarterback of the football team, and class salu-
tatorian.

My love affair with alcohol began in my senior year, after I had
played my last football game. Training and self-denial were over—
now the *fun* could begin! PARTY TIME!

After the first few cans had acclimated my tongue, beer tasted
terrific. So did the camaraderie of friends cruising up and down
the Drag together, shooting pool, and going dancing across the river
in wide-open Louisiana. Remember the exciting and bonding
conspiracy of buying alcohol under age? I can still taste the beer
from the cans we passed around—opened in celebration, and
shared in friendship. The cold, sparkling foam of brotherhood!

No fun activity seemed incapable of being enhanced by drinking. The summer following graduation, we spent numerous nights
playing poker until dawn. We threw ski parties on the river, with
the laughter of the girls ricocheting off the bayous. Our macho
football crowd even camped out and danced naked in the light of
the full moon. We knew that, soon enough, our fun would end
in work, college, or the military, and we were determined to
celebrate our freedom and friendship before we parted.

I knew that my future lay in continuing with school. Pop was a
pipe fitter and former coal miner; Mom, a housewife and part-time
maid by day, a nurse's aide by night. Like their parents and
grandparents, they had struggled their whole lives to make ends
meet. College, for me, was an attractive escape route from this
heritage. The only real question was whether to go party or study.

Knowing that I was capable of either, I purposely chose a challenging academic environment supposedly free of temptation.
Rice University gave me both a scholarship and all that I had
bargained for intellectually. Every student had excelled in high
school. National Merit scholars roamed the campus.

The competitor in me came out in full force. I took dead aim at
the Honor Roll—I *had* to make it. My college friends had the same
ambition. We all studied feverishly, driven as much by fear of
embarrassment as by the desire to succeed. Everyone was accus-
tomed to being top dog. Some now would end up in the middle,
others at the bottom. The *bottom?* Unthinkable!

I remember the day that the first test grades were posted in freshman chemistry. I made a 24 out of 100. I was horrified. Then I learned that the highest score in our class of a hundred students had been a 42, and the average was a mere 18. A couple of my friends had actually scored below 10.

Nothing could have done a quicker job of convincing us cocky eighteen-year-olds that we weren't God's gift to the universe after all. Until then, most of us had never met anybody we couldn't outscore no matter how hard we tried. Suddenly, here was an entire group of us feeling outgunned.

Two things about humility—you either have some or you are going to get some. I learned humility about my intelligence then, but I never dreamed I would later learn humility about alcohol.

## I'll Have What the Gentleman on the Floor Is Having

Drinking in college was fun. We would study fiercely all week, then cut loose with "beer mattress parties" on weekends. Here's how it worked: A student organization would rent a barn outside the city, hire a band, and provide a bunch of kegs. We would then haul scores of cheap dormitory mattresses out to the site, lay them against the barn's interior walls on the perimeter of a dirt dance floor, and drink and dance till we dropped.

Besides relieving tension, I found alcohol made it easier to relax with a date. Raised a strict Catholic, I'd been taught that even French kissing was a mortal sin that would condemn me to eternal hell. The tug-of-war between these teachings of my childhood and the hormones of my adolescence reached a climax in college.

In my innocence, I truly believed that sex before marriage was immoral and that its beauty and significance were tainted without that sanctification. As a result, I broke down in tears the first time I gently stroked my girlfriend's breast.

In retrospect, the beauty and power of love was mesmerizing while we were virgins. We would sit under the stars for hours and stare into each other's eyes, enchanted by mutual promises of love and the belief that its magic would last forever. We would kneel naked in a secluded dorm room, bathed in candlelight, and touch each other wondrously . . . lovingly . . . gently, our spirits soaring in mutual love that reached out and caressed the very universe.

But of course this passionate purity couldn't last. Kids playing with matches could never dream of starting fires so intense. The raging inner conflict between faith and hormones was eventually resolved in favor of the urgings of nature, with the grateful and indispensable assistance of alcohol.

In the years that followed, I don't recall ever going on a date or making love without alcohol being an intimate part of the romantic occasion. We toasted wineglasses by candlelight, sipped champagne in front of a crackling winter fire, washed down barbecue in the hot summer sun with ice-cold beer, and refreshed the tongue with frozen margaritas after spicy Mexican food.

It wasn't that alcohol was a necessity; it just made every occasion seem that much more fun. It also made "making moves" on a date a lot less awkward.

Alcohol also lubricated our group activities. We skinny-dipped at the lake and in the university president's pool. We swam in the public fountains on Houston's Main Street and were chased out by the police. We danced in clubs, frolicked on Mustang Beach, screamed during football games, and stayed up all night while playing in a rugby tournament—all in no pain, pleasurably anesthetized by our favorite brew.

Drinking was fun, relaxing, social, ubiquitous, and virtually problem-free.

## You Can Always Tell an Alcoholic . . . but You Can't Tell 'Em Much

Both during high school and college, I had the occasional friend who drank so much that the rest of us recognized he had a drinking problem. One of our high school buddies, for instance, drank a case of beer every weekend during the summer after graduation. We whispered to each other that he was drinking way too much and might be an alcoholic. In college, I knew a couple of guys who drank until they were toasted nearly every night.

In such situations, we all thought the amount of alcohol being consumed was abnormal, and we made friendly comments to them about our concerns. Then we wrote it off as boys being boys, particularly when they had just relished freedom and had no parental figure around to squelch their fun. We figured they would probably tire of carousing after a while. Failing that, work responsibilities or exams would inevitably pull their chain.

I recall reading during that time that alcoholism was a disease. *What a cop-out!* I thought. *Some guy makes a habit of drinking way too much and wants to blame his behavior on* illness? *Tell him to stop drinking so damn much! Nobody is forcing the alcohol down his throat.*

With minor exception, most of us drank normally, at least by college standards. We would study during the week, then party on weekends and special occasions like birthdays and holidays.

### No Hay Problema

But even we normal drinkers would experience some problems with alcohol. Throwing up occasionally was one. Yet there were apparent reasons for that. It didn't take us long to discover not to drink on an empty stomach. Or to learn that "beer after whiskey was mighty risky; whiskey after beer, never fear."

One of the most unpleasant sensations was to lie down after overindulging, only to feel the room spinning round every time you closed your eyes. The sole remedy was to stay awake until it passed.

College and graduate school were a time not only of learning, but also of experimenting. Simply drinking great-tasting beer, many brands of which had at first tasted lousy, soon wasn't enough. A person had to be more sophisticated, which made it important to learn to drink Scotch. But that presented a problem—the stuff tasted terrible. And unlike other liquors that richly deserved the moniker "firewater," it was not proper to mix Scotch with a soft drink.

Luckily, a friend had a proven method for acquiring a fondness. "Buy a bottle of Cutty Sark," she advised. "Wrinkle up your nose, and drink it over time until you finish the bottle. After that, you'll love the taste." And she was right. It took two weeks to finish the nasty stuff, but I loved it after that.

# 2

## DENIAL IS NOT A RIVER IN EGYPT

◪

Once out in the real world, I continued to enjoy drinking for many years. At first, it was mostly on weekends and other special occasions. Then some coworkers invited me to join them for a drink after work one Thursday. That proved such fun that we made it a regular event. A bar nearby ensured that we'd see friends we would otherwise miss. When *Monday Night Football* began, a lot of us guys would get together to watch, drink, and cheer. That left only Tuesday and Wednesday.

Eventually, Tuesday became a day to have a drink with a friend. And then it became, in addition, a good time to have a little "hair of the dog," for something was needed to cure the hangover generated by celebrations now running from Thursday through Monday.

Pretty soon, Wednesday night ended up a drinking night, too. I'd find myself drinking after work with friends at a bar, with a date at dinner, or with the dog while watching TV.

I might have turned into a pudge with all these empty calories, but fortunately I was fairly vain. To look good, I would lift weights after work several days a week, followed by a three- to five-mile jog around the local lake. Many days, while sweating the previous night's beer out of my system, I'd wonder just how much faster I might fly down the running trail if I weren't drinking.

Because of the drink calories and the added food I ate to counter my worst hangovers, I'd also diet occasionally to shed a few extra pounds. Although none of the diets prescribed alcohol, I logically modified their recommended regimen to include two glasses of low-calorie Chablis a day and found that I could still achieve the predicted weight loss.

During this period, I was in the early years of my legal career and routinely worked long hours. The accompanying stress created a need for the relief afforded by exercise and alcohol. The harder I worked, the more alcohol I'd consume, although during intensive projects, I'd hardly drink at all—perhaps a glass of wine or two to help me fall asleep.

In due time, the long work hours and drinking caught up with me. I didn't know what was going on. All I knew was that I often felt exhausted. I was also experiencing some numbness down my arms, which really frightened me. I went to several doctors to be sure I didn't have a heart problem—and here I was only in my late twenties! Though I was still running regularly and lifting weights whenever I could, increasing my level of exercise to feel better proved no solution. Things got so bad at times that I'd want to hospitalize myself for exhaustion. It never dawned on me that this popular "treatment of the stars" might be medically indicated because of my drinking.

At the time, thanks to a lawsuit I was working on, I was chasing the ghost of Howard Hughes all over the western United States, interviewing people who had known him. It was a fascinating time—talking with John Wayne on the back patio of his Newport Beach house, discovering through Hughes's documents confiscated in Acapulco that the reclusive billionaire was an intravenous codeine addict, and listening to the then unbelievable descriptions by his former servants of a long-haired, naked, paranoid man.

When our scattered legal staff was temporarily united in the same city, I learned the art of drinking Chateauneuf du Pape, Bordeaux, and other fine wines, and to discern which bottle complemented each dish. Thoughts of buying good young wine in quantity and harvesting an excellent wine cellar years later entranced me. I even bought a couple of cases for that very purpose, no bottle of which aged more than three months! I also learned to drink gin—the best, of course. Bombay gin on the rocks, garnished with a skewer of tiny marinated onions, became my favorite hors d'oeuvre.

It seemed all I ever did was work, drink, and sleep. Of course, the sleep was not truly restful because my body was occupied each night processing the latest refill of alcohol. So my exhaustion was actually resulting from sleep deprivation. But that wasn't all.

Because I didn't feel good and my body was hurting, I started experiencing sporadic heart palpitations and anxiety attacks.

A doctor diagnosed my exhaustion and occasional anxiety as being stress-related. His prescription? Valium for relaxation. I was working long hours on the road, so the diagnosis seemed reasonable. My doctor, however, didn't know how much I was drinking in the evenings, in part because I truly wasn't conscious of the amount, and also because I told him I drank "socially—a couple of drinks a night on average."

The truth was, I was averaging four to five drinks a night. I discovered this when I began counting my daily alcohol intake. I had begun running daily, but I was still experiencing destructive hangovers. So I limited myself to no more than two mixed drinks or three beers or glasses of wine a night. I still have the running calendar from the year in which I ran a thousand miles and recorded my daily mileage, the weather, the terrain, *and my alcohol intake.*

A typical entry: "Cool, sunny day. 5 1/2 miles with 2 in the hills. Sluggish at first, gliding at the end. 2 Scotches. 2 beers." By the way, note what's happened to my "limit."

It's incredible, in retrospect, that I did not realize the extent of the challenge that faced me. I thought I was a normal drinker who needed to slow down. The truth is that *no normal drinker finds it necessary to regularly count his alcohol consumption.*

## The Great Fog Machine

While enjoying the nectar of the gods, I knew that drinking hurt my body at times. But I was still unaware that its cumulative effect included an undercurrent of low-level exhaustion. And I certainly would never have guessed that it was also causing an imperceptible disturbance in my brain. Alcohol was affecting my very perception.

"You are like a person driving down a highway at night with your parking lights on," a friend once told me. "There are people who have their headlights on—and some even their high beams." I had no idea what he meant; I just knew life was a struggle.

Alcohol is tricky because it affects your ability to see without your knowing that your sight has changed. The perception of the brain, the instrument that really "sees," has been altered by a regular intake of alcohol, and the brain does not know that it is seeing a modified reality. In other words, alcohol creates its own invisible fog that hides the impact it is having. Its effect is like arrogance in that an arrogant person is the last to discover he possesses that quality. Its very existence hides that trait from the person who has it.

Hoping to see better, I began a journal and inscribed its cover with a life-exploring mission: *"Dedicated to today so that the thoughts and lessons of yesterday can flower and bear fruit."*

In journaling, I noticed that I still savored the companionship and elegance of alcohol. As with many drinkers with successful careers, I got to enjoy alcohol in some posh places. For example, I had the chance to sip Courvoisier VSOP cognac in Amsterdam's Hotel Corona, where it was served by elderly tuxedo-clad waiters in an exquisite Dutch atmosphere of dark mahogany walls, white cloth-covered tables, and lace-embroidered curtains. Inevitably, alcohol soon became associated in my mind with a comfortable, refined lifestyle.

*"When I get back from Holland,"* I wrote in between drinks, *"I'm moving to a cozy home with my antiques, hang the handmade lace curtains and Douglas Whitfield paintings, open my bottle of Dom Perignon, and listen to music. It must have a fireplace and a wet bar! And must be near good running territory."*

But the joy carried a tiresome price: *"Last night I ate in the elegant Hotel Corona dining room and consumed four Courvoisier VSOPs before a four-course sumptuous meal of fresh, unpickled, uncooked herring, veal, potatoes, carrots, peas, clear hot vegetable soup, salad, and dessert, with lots of black steaming coffee from a pot on the table."*

The combination of excessive cognac and coffee left me feeling so bad that the next day I implored in my journal:

*Please, Bert:*

> *Do not drink any more coffee or caffeinated tea or alcohol other than beer.*

*Even to take the edge off loneliness.*
*Your body can recuperate only so often.*

Yet within days, the romance was back: *"Quaffing a half-liter at the sidewalk brasserie at the Arc de Triomphe on the Champs Élysées. The sky is hazy overcast at noon with a touch of chill in the breeze in late August. Un verre de vin rouge, s'il vous plait."*

In the midst of this roller-coaster of merriment and torment, I reflected on my recent loss of a girlfriend: *"Women have been on my mind since I arrived in Europe. Women are seemingly always on my mind, but now I am without one altogether as my last one said that she never wanted to see me again just before I left on vacation. That parting was one I had feared for a long time; surprisingly, at this moment it doesn't feel unsatisfactory in the least. For the first time in my life, I intend to remain free until something really special happens, until a very desired person comes into my life. I am no longer willing to burn time as if it does not exist."*

At times, life felt like a puzzle—and my heart a veritable mishmash of feelings. On leaving Paris, I traveled back to the Dutch province in which I was born, and was unexpectedly overcome by emotion: *"Reading a novel on the train to Maastricht, I glance at the Dutch countryside and feel tears welling in my eyes. Why? Is it because I am alone? Because I am always alone? Because I left here alone and am coming back alone?"*

My solution to loneliness? A woman, of course: *"I want to find a smart, pretty, funny, sexy, honest, caring woman with great legs. Also, don't leave out a desire to have kids. And don't forget to live to be 100 years old to find such a woman! No—I absolutely, categorically refuse to believe that."*

In the murkiness that was my mind, I perceived a connection between my deep desire for love and my use of alcohol:

*I have brains, which is supposed to be advantageous.*
*But this mind, which is so useful professionally,*
*becomes such an albatross in my spare time. And*
*that's why I drink: to still my brain. But eventually*
*alcohol will kill my brain, and there's the rub.*

*But the dream is possible! My equal exists. We will
find each other. Just be faithful to self.*

*It will no longer be necessary to alter reality with
alcohol in order to suppress the thought that my dream
is an impossibility and to soothe the pain of surrender.*

*And remember, you are only looking for <u>one</u>.*

## Insanity Is Doing the Same Thing Over and Over While Expecting a Different Result

During this time I dated some of the most beautiful women on earth. I was single, athletic, articulate, and attractive. I told myself that I was looking for a wife, but my behavior indicated otherwise. All I really wanted was to have a good time. I would take a date to a fine restaurant, toss down a couple of Scotch-and-sodas with my appetizer, have a bottle of wine with dinner, and perhaps enjoy a cognac as dessert. And I do mean that *I* would have a bottle of wine. Most of the women I dated did not drink much. Many were runners I'd met on the jogging trail, and their interest in alcohol was limited to a glass of wine. So during dinner I found myself sucking down the rest of the bottle, which, of course, was fine with me. And if we skipped the predinner drinks, often I would order a second bottle and drink half of it as well. Luckily, I had the ability to remain articulate while intoxicated, and so people rarely suspected that I might be overdrinking.

I was also able to drive well drunk. I vividly remember one outlandish occasion. The lakes and hills around Austin were especially dazzling that night—the silver moonbeams splitting the black water, and the blinking stars seemingly within reach of the sunroof of my new red Porsche. I was racing around sharp curves and jumping over hills, accompanied by a totally naked brunette wearing spanking new store-bought breasts, who was singing and squealing and bouncing through the night. In my mind's eye, I suddenly imagined a headline in the morning's paper: "Drunk President of Young Lawyers Arrested with Naked Woman." But that was quickly followed by a surge of pleasure and, "Oh, what the hell!"

My various women friends never realized that I had a problem with alcohol. Each thought that I celebrated only when I was on a date with her, perhaps because she only drank while out with me, and she assumed that I was doing the same. In truth, I was drinking nightly and was beginning to pay for it with major hangovers.

At work during the week, I found myself getting increasingly impatient for 5:30 to arrive. Many afternoons I painfully watched the clock, awaiting the time when I could down a few quick beers to stop the aching in my head and chest. And that's exactly what I did as soon as I got home—or even on the way home, after a hasty stop at the convenience store if I was feeling particularly bad. The remedy usually worked, although my initial two beers would ordinarily be followed by another two, perpetuating the situation until the next day and starting the cycle all over again.

Weekends were even worse. I controlled my drinking during the week because of work, but on Friday nights I could let go and party. Margarita time! Followed, of course, by a half-dozen beers for good measure. All the worries of work and cares of life were blissfully washed away.

But Saturday morning would come, and I would find myself incapacitated by a hangover. On several such occasions, I made solemn resolutions never to do it again. When those failed, I recorded my agony in the journal so that my crazy amnesiac mind could recall my body's suffering after the pain was gone and another Friday Happy Hour was at hand. Here's one such entry— a particularly disturbing one:

> *The day after being inebriated is hell on earth. My body feels like it will die any minute. My chest cavity has a dull, constant ache. Sometimes my heart skips. Aspirin affords no relief. Sleep is the only real answer, but I am unable to make myself sleep during the day. The digesting of meals taxes and tires and depletes the body's energy even more. The dull ache spreads and becomes more intense as the day passes. Only sufficient alcohol at night stops the body's scream for relief from the awful aching. A tapered dose of alcohol with a prayer that sleep will bring rest and peace, not death in the night.*

I would continue to drink for *five more years* after writing that entry. Why? You tell me. Seriously! Let's examine my thought process in the aftermath of that entry and maybe one of us will understand it.

The very next Tuesday, I wrote: *"Taking care of myself feels real good. Have not had a drink since Saturday. Running is next."*

Two days later, my journal states: *"Ran 4 yesterday and 3 today."* So far, so good.

The next week: *"Did not drink for one week. Nice. Limiting intake now. Doesn't make me feel good now even when I am consuming alcohol."*

What's going on here? I feel good when not drinking for three days, and even better when it's been a week. But then I begin "limiting intake now." Why start at all when it makes me feel so bad?

The very next day after "limiting intake now," I am writing this: *"I'm feeling tired because I drank wine last night and stayed up late. Hope tonight's soccer game and sleep will cure it. My body really needs lots of rest."*

And three days later: *"Sick since the night of the soccer game. Drank beer and smoked cigarettes right after the game."*

My "limited intake" has quickly become a late night of drinking that saps my energy and causes my body to demand rest. Yet I immediately go out and drink beer to the point where my judgment is so clouded that I smoke cigarettes and get sick from self-inflicted physical abuse.

It would be an entire year before I would write again. A hopeless, disheartening cycle had started whirling, and I declined to report for the *Daily Dervish*. But when I next checked in, it was to offer myself the fruits of some significant introspection: *"I'm afraid that I am psychologically addicted to alcohol. It's interesting to go back and look in this journal and see my repeated promises to myself to quit and my recognition of the harm I do to myself physically and emotionally by hiding in alcohol."*

And if it's a psychological addiction, there must be a psychological cause: *"One of the reasons I drink is that my life is not fulfilling. Making money can't be all there is. It's disappointing to live for work and money and to see no hope for much beyond that. So I escape into inebriation. I also date women who have little to offer or challenge me. It reinforces my world view, discourages me, blinds me to hope, and leaves me in the status quo of making money, being unconsciously very discouraged, and escaping into the fog of alcohol. Such a waste—to wallow in a self-induced fog that obscures possibility, the path to happiness, light and love! I want to be in a wonderful relationship with a bright, beautiful, and nurturing woman, and am willing to risk staring disappointment, rejection, and failure square in the face. I pledge to myself that I will not have a sip of alcohol today. I will deal with today only because otherwise I get frightened."*

My pledge "not to have a sip" failed to survive the night. Here's the next day's entry: *"Because of lack of sleep and much alcohol the night before the pledge, my body crashed around 10:00 last night and I drank 2 Scotch-and-sodas just to have any energy at all."* Then a new pledge: *"No alcohol today."* That day, I *"ran and lifted weights. Wanted glass of wine badly after dinner. Resisted."*

What was going on here? I took up the question with my therapist, and here's what I reported afterward: *"My therapist thinks I'm not ready to give up alcohol.* [A brilliant deduction.] *That I'm psychologically, not physically, addicted because of the lack of physical withdrawal symptoms.* [Sorry, no points for agony unless your hands shake.] *And that I'm not ready to stop drinking because I haven't solved the question of what I'm here to do.* [Just how in the hell am I supposed to solve that riddle sporting my ever-fashionable beer goggles?]"

# 3

## NOW HEAR THIS!

What was I here to do? The sudden violent death of a close friend added considerable urgency to that question for me.

Larry was a handsome, joy-filled man with countless friends. We met one Sunday morning when he knocked on my door and told my sleepy face that he was the new neighbor and had prepared vegetable omelettes, fruit, croissants, Colombian coffee, and mimosas with freshly squeezed orange juice for a patio breakfast; and would my girlfriend and I be interested in joining him?

We became best friends. We lived in a lovely old neighborhood of homes with hardwood floors and yards canopied with majestic oaks. We would sit on the porch for hours and talk about life. When Larry died unexpectedly one Friday night, I was stunned. He was thirty-two.

Being a pallbearer at Larry's funeral the following Tuesday brought me starkly face to face with my own mortality. Looking at the metallic blue coffin, its top covered with sprays of flowers, I saw my own coffin and wanted to know, *What would I be satisfied having done on earth when my time came?* If I could, or when I do, watch my own funeral, <u>*what*</u> will have justified my life? What will have been worthwhile?

*"That question, in more subconscious or cloudy form, has permeated my being for years,"* I wrote in my journal. *"Who am I and why am I here? I have the feeling that I am here to accomplish something great. That feeling has been with me since childhood. Is that a childhood fantasy carried into adulthood and evidenced by my ordinary sinful, drinking, women-chasing, wealth-seeking ways? I hope not.*

"I have lived my life in sinful and unproductive ways, certainly unspiritual ways, and I ask forgiveness for that.

"Lack of pride—humility—and forgoing judgment of others seem to be two key principles to live daily. That and being loving and supportive of others.

"May God forgive my many sins, including those committed today!

"Looking at that coffin, everything is stripped away. Politics, work, property, sex—all are so superficial. Everything is a waste of time, except for giving love and learning what life is about. I want to stay in that mind frame for as long as possible so as not to forget, because the noise of living quickly drowns out reality.

"Two things I must avoid to clear my mind and enable me to advance: alcohol and other people, especially women and sex. I need to quiet the noise in my life. I need to spend time with me.

"I avoid myself with alcohol and with women. It is I that I must find and I must look inside.

"As a benchmark, I will describe my current physical state:

> I drink every day. Today (Sunday) two glasses of champagne, one beer, and one glass of wine. Yesterday, only one beer. Friday, one beer, one margarita and cigarettes. Thursday, in bed with a hangover. Wednesday, more than ten beers and six cigarettes on Halloween.

"The alcohol does not make me feel good. My body hurts. My heart skips. I feel sluggish. I sleep a lot to overcome the alcohol in my system. I do not feel in good health, and I worry about it all the time.

"My face feels and looks puffy, with tired shadows and lines under my eyes. I haven't felt genuinely physically good in months.

"Mentally I'm discouraged about my personal life, although work is fine.

"No alcohol. No people. No sex. Let's see what happens."

## That's the Spirit!

A year later, I continued to "struggle with the thought that nothing is worth accomplishing. That no matter the achievement, *whether as a public servant, career professional, or blue-collar worker, in fact it really does not matter. That is a proposition I need to examine. That capsulates my quest for the purpose of my life."*

What is there that's worth doing?

*"Laying up treasures of land and money is not it, though the comforts and travels and leisures afforded by wealth are freeing of the body, and of the mind and spirit if properly directed.*

*"Becoming great for greatness' sake is not it. The casket will close that chapter immediately and easily. Achieving immortality through accomplishments is a contradiction in terms.*

*"I am left with the spiritual. The only things worth accomplishing have to do with the spirit or in service of Spirit, whatever that is. It involves helping others, even on a physical level with food or clothing, because somehow that affects 'spirit' in me even if it has an exclusively physical effect on the other.*

*"The spiritual can be accomplished as a (heaven forbid) lawyer, a novelist, a public figure, or in any other mode—or in several.*

*"Spirituality is not a pejorative word for the first time in more than a decade. Religion still is. So is church. Bureaucracy, wealth, and power politics basically ruined or hid a good thing.*

*"Pop and Mom have advised me several times to trust God concerning my future and not to worry about it. Not to be overly concerned about what I will do, nor to plan or control, but to let God take over. That really makes me feel good. To live as best I can today, to not try to control what I cannot anyway, to relax and let the Creator surprise me, for I cannot envision the tasks and joys that lie ahead. Those joys will only be there if I let go of the absolutely nonexistent false control I desire to exercise out of fear.*

*"That would be a good experience for me. Just to 'allow' God to take over, which He does anyway. How about: just trust God and relax in His loving arms.*

*"It has been so long since I have trusted God. I quit because the church and its priests, who claimed to represent Him perfectly, proved to be wrong and fraught with the blindness and frailties and prejudices and errors of human beings. That has nothing to do with God.*

*"That has been true since the beginning of the human race. Look at all the murders, wars, and suffering caused in the name of Christ*

by the Catholic bureaucracy, the Protestant bureaucracy, and others. Look, too, at those same acts committed in the name of Judaism, Islam, Hinduism, and seemingly every other religion.

"That is not God. I can love my Creator and trust in Him alone, not anyone claiming to represent Him in human form. Trust in God and relax in His goodness and love and strength.

"Become a bearer of His light. That is something that cannot be earned, but it will be, or can be, given to anyone open to it. All that is needed is to relax and be trusting and do good works. Surely doing good deeds does not necessarily entail drudgery. Certainly the famine workers don't feel that way.

"The reason I find vacationing in Europe or the Caribbean an unfulfilling experience is that I am looking to make me happy, and it may be that the only real way to make me happy is in the attempt to make others happy or in helping others. To give to life— happiness being the natural product of a useful way of living."

## Sex and Spirit

As an adult, my "useful way of living" had been the pursuit of women and money—constantly seeking fulfillment or joy through some woman or some thing, with no clue as to my real hunger or quest. How had I strayed so far off the path?

Then, one day, while running off yet another hangover, I experienced an epiphany: "I realized today that I may have searched all these years to find God in a woman. After a childhood steeped in conservative orthodox theology and genuine striving for perfection in God's eyes, I had rejected my religious past as frustratingly unrealistic.

"Yet my search for a woman has always aimed at beauty, inno-cence, love, perfection, wisdom, intelligence, mercy, understanding, and nurturing—in short, all of the spiritual qualities in which I had been immersed as a child, as an altar boy, and the child who wanted to be the perfect boy that God and Mom expected.

"I was innocent.

"And in that innocence was a perfection of spirit for which my being still longs. To be loved unconditionally. To hold, and nurture, and worship another. To return to our womb of spirit together."

I had not been off the path, after all, but was simply unable to see the nature of my pursuit. I yearned for a love that no human could ever provide.

*"In the inevitable disappointment of searching for perfection in another, I spend a lot of evenings inebriated. <u>My way of denial and avoidance</u>."*

And for the umpteenth time, I exhorted myself to change: *"I want to be happy! To <u>feel great</u>! Or just to feel <u>good</u>. It's been several years since I've felt that way. I'm getting started right <u>now</u>."*

# 4

## YOUR MIND IS LIKE A BAD NEIGHBORHOOD: NEVER GO IN THERE BY YOURSELF

■

My effort to feel better consisted of increased exercise. But despite my running and weight-lifting regimen, my body was not staying healthy. I just didn't feel good much of the time and consulted a doctor. The laboratory tests showed that my body chemistry was off balance because my thyroid was producing slowly and my parathyroids were overactive. Neck surgery was recommended.

The prospect of having a scalpel slice open my throat scared me so much that I consulted a holistic healer. She told me that my body was healthy in its natural state and was reacting to impurities put into the system. It needed purification through a specialized diet, high dosages of vitamins and minerals, and *no alcohol*. On her recommendation, I carried a tackle box of pills everywhere. I'd swallow dozens of capsules and tablets at restaurant meals. Other diners stared at me as if I were some crazed drug addict. That I didn't mind. But how could I stop enjoying even harmless wine for an extended time?

Aid came serendipitously. A woman sought my legal advice about a difficult situation with her husband. She had been sober for many years, but he continued to drink heavily. Something had to give, particularly since his behavior was creating legal and economic difficulties for her.

"How did you quit drinking?" I asked her.

"I began by reading the 'Big Book' of Alcoholics Anonymous some years ago and attending twelve-step meetings. . . . Why do you ask?"

"Uh . . . one of my friends confided in me that he's struggling with alcohol. In fact, he might find a copy of that book interesting."

"I'll get one for you." She smiled.

"Thanks."

The next day, a copy was in my chair with a note: "Hope your 'friend' enjoys it."

Were the quotation marks meant as a wink? To this day, I don't know. Then, I didn't care. I was glad to have the book, took it home, and secretly scoured its pages, looking for me.

While reading, I discovered an unexpected desire—I was actually *hoping* to find myself described in its pages. Like a sick person in the doctor's office, I wanted to be diagnosed with a known condition. The fear of the unknown—and perhaps the unsolvable—had given way to a desire for the reassurance of the treatable and curable. But it was not to be.

Several days later, I wrote: *"I have read the book of Alcoholics Anonymous and realize that although I am troubled by alcohol, I <u>do not fit their description of an alcoholic</u> because I have not gone through the disastrous destructive stages the authors describe as typical. However, <u>that does not mean that I have no problem with alcohol</u>. To the contrary, I need to leave it out of my life so that I don't go through those stages."*

Clearly, reading about alcoholism had not been for naught. I had gained knowledge, self-awareness, and a reaffirmation that alcohol and I needed to part company. The problem is that *knowledge and self-awareness alone are absolutely worthless in fighting addiction.*

A bodily addiction will kick your ass while you're sitting around musing and reasoning and making resolutions. The body has developed a physical craving that is both subtle and powerful. That craving has been present from the very first sip as a genetic predisposition or has gradually developed over a long period of time. Either someone in the family tree has changed the normal body chemistry, or you have used your own body as an alcohol-processing plant for so long that its chemistry has altered to the point where the plant has begun to crave the presence of the raw material itself.

The body and the mind both act as if they would prefer not to survive without access to this raw material, which has become a progressively destructive force. Not only does the body soak up more of the substance than makes good sense to give it, but the mind gradually alters to where it cannot even imagine life without alcohol.

"What will I do for fun?" "Life will be boring." "Life will not be worth living." These are insane statements to a normal person, but they appear perfectly rational—indeed *absolute truth*—to the alcohol addict.

### Una Mas, por Favor

During the holistic detox program, I didn't drink for three whole weeks. Then came Cozumel . . .

Because our law firm had enjoyed a spectacularly successful year, we decided to reward the staff with a Christmas vacation on that enchanting Caribbean island. Oh, the delights! Inviting beaches; clear turquoise waters; schools of tropical fish; white sweating frozen margaritas . . .

Some staff members insisted that I drink with them. "Oh, come on, Mr. Pluymen!" they chorused. "You're on vacation!" I had been good for three weeks and my thyroid had healed, but I still faced throat surgery to remove a swollen parathyroid gland, and no amount of abstinence would hold off the knife . . . so what the hell.

Other than making me feel queasy while scuba diving, my nightly drinking was rather uneventful at first. One of our women friends, though, provided plenty of drama. After Lisa drank at dinner the first night, her husband firmly refused to join us at the disco across the street. He went back to our hotel, despite several of the women playfully grabbing his arms and pretending to pull him inside. Once at the disco, Lisa had a few more drinks, then began flirting aggressively with one of the locals, hanging all over him on the dance floor in front of our group. After several dances, she came back toward the couches we were sitting on, forgot about the coffee table holding our drinks, and went sprawling. Everybody laughed louder than sympathy dictated, and Lisa giggled apologetically. A few songs later, her admirer came by for another dance. She popped up, forgot the coffee table again, and planted her face on the floor. No one laughed.

Later, Lisa repeated the performance on the dance floor, without the benefit of a table.

When she appeared on the beach late the next morning, severe bruises were beginning to show on her arms and legs.

"Lisa, can we talk a minute?" I asked, taking her aside under a palm-thatched cabana.

"What's up?"

"Are you OK?"

"Sure, I'm a little hungry, that's all."

"No, Lisa. I'm talking about last night . . . the bruises on your arms."

"Oh, it was dark in there, and I just tripped over the coffee table."

"No, darling. All of us walked by that table just fine. You were falling all over the place."

"I tripped. It could have happened to anybody."

"Yeah, anybody drunk on their butt," I said, laughing. "Look, Lisa, I'm going to tell you something I've never told anybody—I struggle with drinking myself. I stopped for a while, but now I'm drinking again. I watch how much I drink. I know it's tough. Unfortunately, I know what it's like—and you've *clearly* got a drinking problem. You were all over this guy last night, in between crashing to the floor. It's obvious to everybody." I put my arm around her and gently said, "Just look at your arms and legs, Lisa."

"I know," she whispered. "My dad's been sober for five years now. And he's been real worried about me."

In the days that followed, I got to put on some shows of my own. I was a gas—turning full margarita schooners upside down on the restaurant dinner table to trap the frozen concoction inside, laughing uproariously while pouring a drink over a friend's head, being paid back with a piña colada inside the front of my drawers, loudly demanding that an overweight staff member stop eating her Mexican food immediately, and generously tipping the restaurant staff for all the commotion. Apart from a few oppressive hang-overs, it was riotous fun.

On returning home from vacation to face surgery, I became fearful because an operation raised all my control issues to their highest degree. I prayed more than I had in years and climbed onto the water wagon for a week. Gratefully, surgery turned out to be successful, and my continued presence on the wagon during two weeks of recovery was surprisingly easy. In fact, I proudly announced in my journal: *"The compulsion to drink is not there. I can take it or leave it."* Then I threw a party to celebrate my newfound health and freedom.

## Desperado

My journal entry the next day is among the most revealing I've ever penned: *"Had a party last night and am skipping tonight's black-tie, roof-top, New Year's Eve blowout because I am in terrible pain. I am severely hungover, my chest hurts, and my heartbeat has been palpable all day. It's really not at all pleasant. And neither was last night.*

*"I am not capable of enjoying myself.*

*"I had begun to think I could drink and have fun, but that does not appear to be the case. This misery has gone on for far too many years. It does not serve me and stands as a block to my fulfillment.*

*"I want to make a contribution in life, to do something significant for people. Maybe the reason people become alcoholics is that, at their core, they don't feel they are contributing anything really worthwhile despite external appearances, and they drink in disappointment of themselves to cover a despair—a quiet, deep despair that this is all there is. Could alcoholics be hard-core dreamers from childhood who subconsciously realized that they are not able to achieve great things on their own, and that even if they did, death will quickly snuff the flicker anyway? Is that why spirituality appears as the only answer to the hopelessness of alcoholism?*

*"Drinking has gone beyond a habit, to a craving. <u>Knowing why I drink is truly not relevant</u>. All that matters is that I continue in spite of the knowledge that drinking is hurting me, and that I drink regardless of my strong desire to quit. <u>I am destroying myself against my own will</u>."*

Desperately wanting to break the cycle, I recalled that I had twice interrupted it on doctor's orders. Was I capable of staying away from alcohol voluntarily for a week?

Definitely!

But I found it necessary to talk myself out of a beer or glass of wine every night. That scared me enough that I decided to leave alcohol alone for a whole month to prove to myself that I was *not* an alcoholic.

The first four days of combating the desire for alcohol were, as always, the most challenging—mentally, emotionally, and physically. After that, the going was easy. "Obviously," I cheerfully concluded, "alcohol is not a true addiction for me."

In fact, the month had been so effortless that I resolved to continue without alcohol on weekdays, but would allow myself to enjoy it with friends at Friday Happy Hour and Saturday night out. No problem!

Two weeks later, I realized that I had consumed some type of alcohol every night since my "weekend only" proclamation. Apparently, I was so relieved to be able to drink again that I subconsciously slipped back into my old pattern, oblivious to my broken pledge. So I resolved to go *two* months without alcohol. That successful effort was followed by another failed "I will now drink only occasionally" declaration. Annoyed, I finally sentenced myself to a *three*-month summer abstinence—and the effects were magical:

*"Just ran and meditated in the morning and feel physically and mentally great. Physical exercise without alcohol makes me feel wonderful. It's really amazing that I ever drink since I feel so good without it.*

*"In the last 3 1/2 months, I have danced till 4:00 in the morning, slept in, and felt just fine. I have worked out at the YMCA on Saturday mornings, feeling great, while listening to the moaning and groaning of the alcohol partyers attempting to recover from the night before. I have gone to one political function after another, cocktail party after party, and various bars and nightclubs without the thought or desire of a drink. I have been able to work with a clear and active mind and lots of energy."*

And my sobriety coincided with a spiritual awakening: *"God has been very good to me. Whenever I ask something, it has been given. When I look for the presence of Spirit now on a daily basis, I see it working and recognize its presence. It has been hard in the past to believe that God is so personal a being or that God would care about me in such a personal way."*

Life sounds wonderful, doesn't it? But guess what? *I let it all go . . . and I don't know why.* My excuses included the tension of a major trial and the lure of a bodacious redhead I'd met at a local club near closing time, when I was the only articulate guy left because I was sober.

A month later, to escape the pressure cooker of trial work, I rendezvoused with Ms. Red in France. It proved disastrous. After drinking under the stars at a sidewalk café in Nice, we walked arm in arm over the cobblestones to our hotel and awoke squinting at each other in the bright morning light.

"Oh, your legs are so brown," observed she, gently stroking his tanned thigh.

"Your hair is fire red," replied he, twirling a few strands between his fingers.

"Told you I was a real redhead."

After that, we had absolutely nothing else to say to each other. A long train ride later, and the narrow streets of Venice pressed in to choke the life out of me. How could such an overwhelmingly sensual city be so stifling, especially when you're accompanied by a stunning woman?

*"What have I silently decided?"* I wrote in Italy. *"That sex is paramount? That breasts and nice legs are all that count? That making lots of money is the only career goal? No wonder you like to drink alcohol or caffeine or smoke cigarettes or work or exercise excessively. Stop!"*

Stopping and starting drinking is like driving in and out of a swirling mist: *"Right now I feel like I'm going through life as if I'm in a fog. It is so difficult to see clearly, to think clearly about my life and its meaning. Why is it all so confusing? Why is it so difficult to remember experiences clearly and translate them into effective learning experiences?"*

From the outside, the answer is obvious; but on the inside, I found myself asking: *"Is this a function of alcohol or is this life? I risk that question even though it likely would give someone the wrong idea about my alcohol consumption, which at its worst has never averaged more than five drinks a day, which is bad enough.*

"When I spend time with some people, I am surprised at how much I see that they miss. The matters I see quickly and clearly are not noticeable to them without some difficulty. Blessed are those whose eyes can see so much more than mine, whose perception concerning the truly important things in life is clear and strong."

# 5

## THIRTY MINUTES OF BEGGING
## IS NOT FOREPLAY

My perceptions concerning life were anything but clear and strong. After taking the sworn testimony of a hand surgeon until late one night, I stopped at a quiet bar to resuscitate. The place was empty and the beer was cold. The waitress was pretty, friendly, and blonde. We talked and laughed about sailing and running and life. She was no longer interested in her old boyfriend, and sure, she would love to jog the next day.

As the ducks and swans rode the ripples of Austin's Town Lake, we ran through the trees along the water's edge, confiding our most intimate secrets while becoming closer stride by stride. On the crest of a hill, she suddenly stopped and said, "Look, there's something I want you to know about me. I don't know if it's me . . . or the guys I pick. But my deepest desire is to be able to stay committed in a relationship, and I just can't seem to make myself do that."

Looking into the blue eyes of this gorgeous woman, whom I'll call Kristen, all I could see was beauty and innocence. And honesty. On the spot, I fell in love. Or, more accurately, dove into addiction.

It was clear from the first that I had no boundaries. In picking her up from work, I often waited on bar stools and in parking lots for an hour until she closed her final tab. Or I'd count the minutes at home after she called at midnight to say she was going for a drink with another waitress, and would be over shortly, only to come rolling in at three.

Like most abnormal drinkers, I had lived my life down to a pencil point. The road had once been wide and filled with promise and opportunity. Earlier, at age thirty-two, I had friends call and leave seemingly joking messages congratulating me on becoming a legal celebrity. I wouldn't believe them until I'd seen the book they'd bought, called *The Best Lawyers in America,* by Harvard Law grads Naifeh and Smith. There was my name, keeping company with the most famous attorneys in the land, many of whom were grizzled warriors. Not bad for an immigrant kid who, at age ten, had to fight his way into American grammar school because the resident bully refused to let him set foot on the school grounds. But that was then, and this was now. "Now" meant a gorgeous home on a cliff, with the twinkling lights of Austin carpeted for miles below, with the occasional deer grazing outside the picture windows, and a lonely man drinking Glenlivet, waiting for the only person in his life to come over. No men friends. No group of friends who socialized together. No life outside of this woman, or the one before her.

Kristen went out often with girlfriends, or so she claimed. I certainly didn't mind, but her stories sometimes made no sense, especially on weekends. So early one Saturday morning, I walked into her house without knocking and extended my hand to the surprised stranger standing in the kitchen, while she sat dumbfounded at the table.

"Hi, I'm Bert."

"Hello, I'm Darren."

The name belonged to her old boyfriend, and I turned and walked out, knowing the truth.

"You shall know the truth, and the truth shall set you free," says the Gospel. The writer should have added "unless you are addicted." The following week, I was back for more. Dropping in at her workplace, I professed my undying love and desire to keep seeing each other. She accommodated. How amazing that she would continue dating someone this stupid.

The painful cycle continued. We spent a romantic ski holiday in Snowmass, with thick flakes drifting onto forests of aspen by day, and firelight flickering over lovers aglow from Bordeaux at night. I wanted the magic to last forever. Kristen insisted on leaving early—and could not be reached at home that night.

Foolishly unable to accept that she simply wasn't in love, I figured her behavior had to be prompted by her partying, because the two seemed to coincide. So after another evening escapade, I confronted her one morning and told her that she was a wonderful, kind, and caring person when sober, but that once she'd consumed alcohol, our relationship meant nothing. I could not continue to hurt as I did, and she would have to choose between me and alcohol. I was out of her life if she continued to drink.

Kristen started crying, saying she didn't want to lose me, and up and quit on the spot. At noon, I accompanied her to an AA meeting because, in my mind, *she* obviously needed it. But I was real curious about my own drinking and wondered whether I would meet my kith and kin.

## Put a Fork in Me, I'm Done

The inconspicuous building was surrounded by Spanish oaks and appeared to be a spacious house. The meeting room itself was dark and smoky, though divided between smokers and nonsmokers. The person in front talked about his alcoholism and called on others to speak. One guy with multiple tattoos mentioned spending three terms in the state penitentiary, the last for armed robbery. Another described sitting in a roadside park, drinking whiskey out of a brown paper sack. *No, AA was not for me.*

But neither was drinking. I was beginning to discover that for me, like many people, there is no middle ground. You have to either go one way or the other. Either not drink at all or drink to excess. It's like driving down the road and coming to a fork. You can either take the left or the right fork. You have no choice to keep going straight.

The fork was fast approaching for me.

Kristen and I had enjoyed partying together. We had spent glorious weekends on the sailboat, playing naked in the sun, drinking wine coolers, and sleeping under the stars. We had enjoyed the sensation of pouring wine down each other's throats until it overflowed, bathing us in the liquid, and making love. It never occurred to me that I had not made love completely sober in my entire life.

At restaurants or bars, I often ordered two beers when first sitting down, because invariably the first bottle was finished long before

the waiter checked our table again. And my best friends were people who could keep up with me. It was real special to watch *Monday Night Football* with a friend who drank beer as fast as I did.

"Are you ready for another one?"

"You bet."

I knew I had a problem with alcohol, but was not ready for the
solution. I distinctly remember a billboard in town that depicted
the chalked outline of a body. The caption read, "What will it
take?" And I knew *exactly* what it was talking about.

Yet there were times when I could choose the dry fork of the
road for months. One time, because of boredom with law, I
temporarily lost my sanity and ran for mayor. Knowing that my
mind needed to be clear as a bell, I simply avoided alcohol for six
months. But that's all I did. I was incapable of making other
fundamental changes in my life, such as letting go of an inappro-
priate relationship—because I had no mechanics for doing so.

Meanwhile, Kristen continued to indicate that she was unhappy
being with me. After we became engaged, she briefly broke off our
relationship before deciding to go through with the wedding. For
my part, my fantasy and addiction remained intact. I was elated
when we married and still blindly in love.

My other addiction, to alcohol, was relatively under control, in
part from living with Kristen, who no longer drank. Many times, I
would go a couple of weeks without anything myself. Then I'd
find her immersed in studying for exams or writing a paper, and I
would keep myself company by drinking a six-pack or a bottle of
wine while watching television.

There were also times, after having a few drinks, when I'd get an
urge to *bathe* in alcohol. Not only drink it, but actually sit in it and
splash it over my body and under my arms. It was like an impulse
that emerged from the back of my mind, enticing me to just let go
and swim in the stuff. I never yielded to that urge, but I did have
to fight it. It felt as though the day would come that I would
inevitably surrender to its seductive call. Coincidentally, I had
repeated water dreams, in which I would be walking along the
steep bank of a raging river, accidentally slide down the muddy
slope, and be hurtled downstream in the rushing waters, simultaneously frightened and exhilarated.

Six months into the marriage and ten days since my last drink,

I had a crucial court date out of town. I was anxious about the hearing because a loss would cause the dismissal of my client's case and expose an embarrassingly dumb legal decision by me. The night before the hearing, I dined with my law partner and his wife, and drank two glasses of chardonnay, in part to still my fear of impending doom. Then he and I departed directly to the airport, where we awaited our flight in—where else?—the bar. There we discussed the published cases that hopefully would influence the judge in our favor. For reference purposes, I removed these prior court decisions from my briefcase and laid them on our table in the airport bar. After I'd had two glasses of wine, our flight was called and we departed . . . without the critical material.

Realizing my blunder at the hotel that night, I frantically called lawyer friends at our destination to gain access to a law library at dawn. That desperate task accomplished, I fell into a fitful sleep. In the morning, the favorable cases were again located, the judge ruled in our favor, and we happily flew home.

Back at the office that afternoon, my female law partner, who hardly knew my wife, came up and said, "Bert, I had the strangest dream last night."

"What was that, Amanda?"

"I dreamed that Kristen had an affair."

On returning home, I said, "Honey, you wouldn't believe what Amanda dreamed last night."

"What's that?"

"She dreamed you had an affair."

Well, Kristen just turned white as a sheet. Then she stammered, "L-look, that's not true. But we need to talk. . . . I'm not happy . . . and I want to separate."

Instantly, I was in a different world. An unreal place. Another time. My body and mind were disconnected from the room. I was in shock. My heart began beating irregularly. "This just can't be!" I exclaimed. "Why?"

"I just can't do this."

"Is there someone else?"

"No!"

"Please, honey, let's do something . . . Marriage counseling . . . Anything . . . *Please!*"

"I can't."

I began crying softly. Kristen slumped into a chair. I went over, knelt on the floor, held on to her leg, and wept shamelessly, begging her to change her mind. That night she slept in another bedroom. Being unable to sleep, I went in and watched her breathe, gently waking her to ask once more. But she was adamant about leaving.

And she swore up and down that there was no one else.

But, of course, there was, and she was in love with him. And my life would either end in a deluge of alcohol and pain, or my resurrection would begin here. I badly wanted to be raised to a new and different life. How could I be so blind as to not see what was happening right in front of me? How could I so terribly misjudge a relationship? *How could anyone live in such a fantasy world?*

I needed help, and I knew I couldn't do it on my own. So I asked a good friend, who'd been sober three years, to take me to another AA meeting. At noon the next day, we went to a room where people laughed and hugged as they entered. Once inside, they talked about how good life was and how grateful they were. When it was my turn, all I could share was my pain, sobbing uncontrollably. They loved me, held me, and consoled me.

And they told me that the only requirement for membership was a desire to stop drinking—I didn't have to be an alcoholic to join.

Two big guys came up to me after the meeting. One was a building contractor and the other an engineer. Both were going through painful divorces, one with two young boys and the other with three. We fast became inseparable friends.

**PART TWO**

# RECOVERY

You are about to have the most meaningful relationship you will ever have. That relationship is with yourself. You are about to discover who you really are.

—James, a janitor with a fourth-grade education

# 6

## LIE DOWN ON YOUR BACK
## AND YELL, "UNCLE!"

◪

As children, we learned a simple lesson that escapes us as
adults. When pinned to the ground in an excruciating position, we could secure our freedom from pain and constraint merely
by yelling, "Uncle!" Now, as adults, we would rather die than be
humiliated, yet the answer remains the same. We once found
friendship, kindness, and freedom on the other side of surrender.
This very day, indescribable power and grace still flow when we
just let go and have the humility to admit that we are powerless.

An admission of a character defect, and the resulting capitula-
tion to the idea that we are only human, is arduous. Even when we
have more problems than Carter has liver pills, we refuse to
surrender and stubbornly hang on to our old ideas. In drinking, we
want to be like everybody else, and we are willing to die trying.
And often do.

But the simple fact is that we are all different, with various
physical and mental strengths and weaknesses. And some of us
have a physical addiction to a liquid that contains the chemical
compound ethyl alcohol. The only way out is to admit that we
have no power over this ostensibly innocuous substance. And that
is without question the most difficult accomplishment for a strong,
intelligent person: acknowledging that we are different and seemingly admitting that we are weak.

The first step toward recovery is simply to admit that we are powerless over alcohol and that our lives have become unmanageable.
For me, when I was confronted with my greatest fear—unexpected
total abandonment by my true love—I knew instinctively that,

despite years of trying to regulate my alcohol intake, I was power-less over alcohol, and that it would kick my butt if I elected to wallow in it.

But I refused to believe my *life* was unmanageable.

We always think, no matter how bad it gets, that our lives are manageable and normal, because the life we have led to this day is the only one we've ever known, and we inherently believe that life without alcohol would be worse. We have had no experience of what a better life, a really good life, is like. We haven't tasted the joy and freedom that lie ahead.

Once we are well into recovery and our life has improved beyond our fondest dreams—physically, emotionally, and financially—at every moment we still believe that this is as good as it gets. Again, because this is all we know. And with each move to a higher plane, we invariably believe that this is the end of advancement, partic-ularly if it looks and feels great. We are unable to see beyond where we are. We have no experience of being more joy filled, more spiritual, more at peace, and more physically and financially free.

But *beginning* is the most difficult, even though it contains the seed that will grow into a life of fulfillment and happiness. Walk-ing through the doors into an AA meeting is quite a challenge. It takes courage, humility, and a profound commitment to self.

Once there, wonderful surprises await. My first day, I feared being recognized because I felt ashamed. But I immediately found highly accomplished people whom I knew and respected. And seeing them caused an unexpected sensation: I was *proud* of them—and no longer felt ashamed to be seen myself. I was also surprised to see so many young people, even teenagers.

At the meeting, I was told that I had a physical addiction to alcohol, and that decades of experience by millions of people show that it is a progressive disorder. The only known cure is abstinence this day. *I did not need to decide to quit drinking the rest of my life, or even for a week. I only needed to resolve not to drink today. And I could do that.* On Friday night, when I had the urge to drink, I re-solved to go out and get really drunk—on Saturday night. And by Saturday, the desire usually passed. If not, I decided to get snock-ered on Sunday. It was very, very enlightening to discover such urges are passing phenomena that simply change of their own accord if not acted on.

## Wanted: New General Manager of Universe

Even the strongest among us must listen when the voices sing of new directions, new voices, new visions.

—source unknown

In addition to having a physical addiction, I learned that I likely shared some attitudes with other abnormal drinkers, one of them being that I considered myself to be the center of the universe—in fact, its general manager. And that it was time for me to resign from that position. And that the whispers carried on the winds are true—there *is* a higher power than me in the universe, even though I might not believe that or even resent the very idea that I don't sit at the pinnacle of power over an empire some ten billion light-years across. And if I found it impossible to believe in an unseen spirit with power greater than my own, then I could recognize and acknowledge my new group of colleagues with more experience in sobriety as a higher power. I was told that "no one need have difficulty with the spirituality of the program. *Willingness, honesty, and open-mindedness are the essentials of recovery. But these are indispensable.*

There is a principle which is a bar against all informa-tion, which is proof against all arguments and which cannot fail to keep a person in everlasting ignorance— that principle is contempt prior to investigation.

—Herbert Spencer"[1]

Just as bluntly, I was informed that selfishness and self-centered-ness were at the root of our common problem, and that we needed to get rid of this attitude and way of living before it killed us. Self-centeredness led inexorably to self-reliance, which was our navigator on the journey that got us here. Wisdom and guidance untold were available if only we were open to it.

Well, I was open because my personal life was in a shambles.

Kristen and I had gone to weekly marriage counseling during a three-month separation. We'd planned to reconcile our six-month marriage and had just rented a new house to live in together. But the night before the move, I stopped by her apartment for a visit. When she opened the door, it was obvious that here was a different woman. "There's something I need to tell you," she said immediately. "I want a divorce."

My vision momentarily jarred, as if someone had stumbled into a video camera making a recording of my life.

"Tell me what the fuck's been going on!"

"What do you mean?"

"You know what I mean. *Who* is he?"

"I don't know what you're talking about."

"Yes, you do. Come on, Kristen! I'm not stupid. Tell me who it is."

After a long pause, she said, "You're right. I'm in love with a man named Billy, and I want to be with him. For the first time in my life, I know what love is like. I truly hope you find out some day, too." We waited a long time . . . in silence. Then she said, "Bert, if it wasn't him, it would have been somebody else. You and I don't even have a song."

"A song?"

Then she handed me an envelope and said, "Here are my wedding and engagement rings."

Like the foolish romantic I'd always been, I replied, "No, you keep them. Someday, I want you to be able to look back and see that you once had a really good husband." And I walked out with my heart in my throat.

I will forever be grateful to Kristen for following her heart's desire to be with the love of her life. In leaving, she inadvertently rescued me from a painful existence that would only have ended in a much worse place.

But driving around the next day looking for a new place to live—alone—I felt a profound sadness that turned into an occasional tear rolling down my cheek and gradually became raw, unrestrained crying. I called AA Intergroup* and asked for the nearest ongoing meeting, which turned out to be a "men only" gathering at the low-bottom club I had attended with Kristen two years earlier. This time, because I openly shared my grief, the support at the meeting was extraordinary. Human beings are truly at their finest when they reach out and give of themselves to a fellow in need. A meeting is one of the few places on earth where men fearlessly show honest love and support for each other.

Once I became willing and open, magical coincidences began occurring. Emotionally incapable of moving into a house we had chosen together, I promptly found a gingerbread cottage cradled in ivy and live oaks. The owner agreed to move immediately because I had no place to live, and she did something that would have seriously offended me only days before—she sent me cards with supportive biblical quotations:

> The Lord's loving kindnesses never cease.
> For his compassion never fails.
> They are new every morning!
> The Lord is all I have,
> So, I put my hope in Him.
>
> —Lamentations 3:22–24

> Do you not know? Have you not heard?
> The everlasting God,
> The Lord,
> The Creator of the ends of the earth
> Does not become weary or tired!
> He gives strength to the weary
> And to him who lacks might, he increases power!
>
> —Isaiah 40:28–29

---

*Practically every city in the world has a phone book listing for one of many mutual-support groups for sobriety, particularly Alcoholics Anonymous. Others such as Women for Sobriety, Secular Organizations for Sobriety (SOS), and S.M.A.R.T. Recovery are also available in a limited number of communities.

Being in constant pain, I repeatedly read these reassuring words about kindness, compassion, hope, and strength. I know this won't mean much if you have never walked and lived in total darkness, and it may even be laughable or offensive to you. But the day may come when your bare feet will also desperately feel for rock to walk on and be gratefully steadied by the touch of solid ground.

After the initial shock of rejection subsided, my mind obsessed over what went wrong and what I could have, should have, done and said differently. My friends surely became ill listening to my laments—over and over. One suggested a wonderful little book called *How to Survive the Loss of a Love,* which was informative and, gratefully, humorous. Another recommended interrupting my thoughts with prayer. Consequently, I would drive down the expressway, endlessly repeating the Our Father.

During this darkest hour, I received the greatest gift anyone has ever given me. Someone suggested that, first thing every morning, before my mind started running its usual negative tape, I read the 23rd Psalm:

> The Lord is my shepherd; I shall want nothing.
> He makes me lie down in green pastures,
> and leads me besides the waters of peace;
> he renews life within me,
> and for his name's sake guides me in the right path.

Since Judea was mostly an arid and rocky wasteland, with turbulent rushing waters after a rain, it would be a mighty shepherd indeed who could rest his flock in green pastures, next to peaceful waters, lacking nothing.

> Even though I walk through a valley dark as death
> I fear no evil, for thou art with me,
> thy staff and thy crook are my comfort.

Unlike today, once you left a Judean town, you walked into a wilderness with paths through deep ravines—"valleys dark as death"—where thieves, murderers, and natural predators waited to pounce. But a good shepherd carried a sturdy staff—a cudgel for warding off wild animals—as well as a crook for guiding his sheep.

> Thou spreadest a table for me in the sight of my enemies;
> thou hast richly bathed my head with oil,
> and my cup runs over.
> *Goodness and love unfailing, these will follow me*
> *all the days of my life,*
> and I shall dwell in the house of the Lord
> my whole life long [italics added].

So *every morning* I knew that God would ward off the wild beasts in my life that day, while guiding me safely through valleys appearing dark as death. I could let go of my worst fears and trust to be led to peaceful pastures. And, best of all, at a time of feeling totally unloved and alone, I woke up every day assured— assured!—that *goodness and love unfailing would follow me all the days of my life.* To this day, that remains my favorite line in the English language.

Another helpful suggestion made to this proud person was the idea of humbling myself in prayer. A friend offered this recommendation: "Put your car keys under the bed at night so that you have to get down on your knees to get them in the morning, and while you're down there . . ."

As silly as it may sound to any agnostic who has persevered in reading to this point, communicating with the unseen spirit does change things. And you don't have to believe in the unseen spirit, or God, or a higher power, or whatever name you prefer, for it to work. All you have to do is sincerely try it. *You can fake it till you make it.* For example, people struggling with alcohol can get down on their knees, hold out their arms, and honestly say, "I can't keep living like this anymore. And I can't stop alone. Please take this burden from me." Incredibly, the craving to drink will be taken away.

Don't be too proud to try something in the spiritual realm that you don't understand. You do it in the physical world every night when you flip on a light switch, not having any real idea how or why electricity works. You use computers, watch television, and enter relationships, not having a clue as to how any of it works. Why not give yourself the opportunity, in private, to receive the biggest and best surprise gift of your life?

As a famous prince once said to his friend Horatio:

> There are more things in heaven and earth, Horatio,
> Than are dreamt of in your philosophy.
>
> —*Hamlet*

And don't confuse this with "religion." We are talking "spirituality," not religion or church. Plenty of men and women currently addicted to alcohol are good active church members, ministers, or priests.

Some people come to spirituality easily and without preconceived notions or prejudices, and others have to be in the desperate straits of drowning men or women, willing to grasp at anything to survive. And when you find yourself in danger of drowning in alcohol or its consequences, you may reach out and experience what millions before you have:

> What seemed at first a flimsy reed, has proved to be
> the loving and powerful hand of God.[2]

# 7

## HALT

By going to AA meetings and lunch or dinner afterwards, I found new friends who were not only supportive, but experienced and wise. They told me that it was not necessary to believe everything I heard. The program was a buffet of ideas and suggestions, and I could choose what I liked and leave the rest. "Whatever works is what counts," they'd say.

One of the most useful ideas dealt with alleviating known trigger points to drinking. I was told to **HALT** when any one of these arose, because each was a red flag:

**H:** hungry   **A:** angry   **L:** lonely   **T:** tired

My brain could construe the body's longing for food when **hungry** as a craving for alcohol. So any time I was hungry, I needed to stop and eat. This made sense because drinking wine or beer or Scotch or margaritas had certainly let me postpone the need for dinner on numerous occasions, particularly on Friday night. Just as a couple of drinks easily quelled the immediate desire for food, eating promptly satisfied the apparent appetite for a drink.

I was told that being **angry** would create a subconscious urge to drink away this unpleasant feeling, with the resulting conscious attitude of "The hell with it, give me a beer." So whenever I became angry, it was essential that I talk about it right away with the person involved—or, if that was not possible or productive, then with someone willing to listen until the anger was gone. Unlike my experience with partying and hunger, this did not sound familiar.

It reminded me of old black-and-white movies in which a guy would drown his sorrow and rage in a bottle. A nice guy like me didn't get angry and certainly would never think about *drinking* over it.

So it came as quite a surprise when I found myself exasperated at work that the first thought popping into my head was, *I'll stop and get a six-pack on the way home.* Where was this coming from? Apparently, I had anesthetized my feelings with alcohol all those years, and not liking this new sensation—otherwise known as a genuine emotion—my instinct was to get rid of it immediately by any means necessary.

It is no accident that **lonely** people hang out in bars. When I first graduated from law school and had my own apartment, I hated the thought of going to that "empty" place alone. Instead, I would drive to a local watering hole, always populated by a few familiar faces, and join them for a drink. That is one of the wonderful side benefits of alcohol: you can avoid experiencing unpleasant feelings. The trouble is that you miss the growth inherent in processing authentic emotions, and by artificially suppressing them, you stay at the same level of maturity—for years.

My new friends suggested that loneliness is a danger sign for the abnormal drinker, and that quick remedies include interacting with friends by phone or experiencing the companionship of a meeting. A major problem with loneliness is that we have a tendency to start feeling sorry for ourselves when it arises, given our proclivity toward self-centeredness. It's the "poor me" syndrome, which goes, "Poor me, poor me—pour me a drink."

Finally, we know that **tired** people have been known to drink. They don't call them "pick-me-ups" for nothing. At the end of an exhausting day at work or long evening out, the calories in alcohol can provide a welcome lift for a fatigued body and weary mind. But alcohol is, in fact, a depressant rather than a stimulant. The more a person drinks to stimulate energy, the more is needed to overcome the depressant effect. The temporary lift is borrowed from the future, the price being paid later in this zero-sum game. The real solution for being tired is to rest. What a unique concept!

When you're **hungry**, eat. When **angry**, talk. When **lonely**, visit. And when **tired**, rest. Hell, even I could do that.

## Relief

The camaraderie of new friends brought another wise piece of advice. I was told that *there are no more big deals.* That was a source of incredible relief for a guy who could obsess over a problem or situation and make it a life-or-death matter. I was told to do the best I possibly could but to let go of personal accountability for the results.

Before, there was always an undercurrent of anxiety about work and my life. At the office, I felt totally responsible for every detail of each case, an impossible burden when representing a hundred clients. No wonder I drank to relieve stress! Once I realized there was a power in life greater than I, it occurred to me that the vast majority of the details were in the purview of that power. Although I certainly needed to suit up and show up, work diligently, and even battle strenuously when appropriate, it was a tremendous relief to trust that unseen Spirit would take care of the details. I could just envision that power crackling through the files. I know it sounds silly, but there were miraculous outcomes in impossible cases once I took that attitude.

I had always taken life seriously and responsibility very personally—and paid a high price in anxiety. Heart palpitations started in high school and led to occasional mild panic attacks by law school. No matter how much I exercised, my heart would sometimes skip, and its forceful pounding inside my chest would cause me to freeze in terror. Although a heart specialist once tried to reassure me about the harmlessness of premature ventricular contractions, my emotions would run wild when they occurred.

A palpitation started with a seeming pause in the normal heartbeat, followed by a physical blow under the breast bone. I would immediately become hyperalert for any telltale numbness or pain in my chest or arms, and that worry led to hyperventilation, which quickly induced panic mode—the fear and the symptoms rapidly amplifying each other in a process similar to the shriek produced when a microphone is held too close to a loudspeaker. When it happened at home, I would ask a friend to come over right away and be with me until I felt safe. Once it occurred while I was driving down an LA freeway. I pulled my car onto the shoulder and fought the waves of anxiety until they passed. More embarrassingly, I actually jumped out of my car at a local intersection, flagged down another driver, and entreated the stranger, "Please help me. I don't feel good. My heart is skipping, and it really scares me. Please watch me for a little while to make sure I'm OK." Then I had to convince that poor, alarmed Good Samaritan not to call an ambulance. To avoid repeating that embarrassing public spectacle, I have been known to drive to a hospital and sit in the Emergency Room parking lot to be near medical assistance should the irregular beats progress to a heart attack. Fine thing for a guy in his late twenties or early thirties to be doing.

I know old friends and colleagues won't recognize the person I'm describing. But panic attacks were in fact a pretty rare occurrence, as well as a source of shame, for this tough rugby player, who would be fine one moment and the next be terrorized by the unexpected betrayal of his heart.

And you know what? The anxiety attacks have disappeared since I became sober. Heart palpitations don't scare me anymore. For one, *I have faith in the fundamental goodness of the universe* and believe that I'll be just fine. For another, if I'm meant to go now, that is OK with me. And finally, it is apparent that I fostered heart palpitations by my actions, and it is fairly simple to avoid them with a change of behavior. Alcohol and its physically draining aftereffects undoubtedly precipitated most occurrences. Caffeine, lack of sleep, stress-filled living, and lack of exercise were all contributing factors. So when I don't drink, avoid excessive caffeine, say an occasional prayer, sleep normally, and exercise regularly, I feel absolutely great. And that's been the situation since June 2, 1989. Now, who could not do that?

*The person who can't is the one who tries to do it alone.*

It is impossible to describe the fellowship of professional women and men, blue-collar workers, homemakers, African-American men, Junior League women, Native Americans, professors, janitors, Hispanics, athletes, and artists that awaits the person with a desire to stop drinking. From the lonely man who identified with Peggy Lee's "Is This All There Is?" I have become a man blessed with wonderful friends. We know each other well and care about each other deeply, because we share who we really are. My best friends include two struggling teenage boys, a couple of hopeful men just out of prison, a highly successful nightclub owner in the Virgin Islands, a hilarious banker who is a recovering crack addict, a professional athlete who played in three Super Bowls, and some of the finest and most courageous women on earth. Who could pass this up?

# 8

## "YOU'RE NOT AN ALCOHOLIC"

If you choose a high bottom, your friends, family, and coworkers will initially tell you that you don't have a drinking problem. Some will even try to argue you out of being an alcoholic, as if that were possible. But it is not up to them or me or anyone else to decide whether you are or aren't—only you can decide that. And time will tell whether you made the right decision.

My dad was adamant that I was not. Pop doesn't drink and had never witnessed any consequences of my drinking. Because of his love for me, he didn't want to believe that his son was an alcoholic. After one particularly lengthy discussion, he suggested that it was all right for me to drink; I should just limit myself to a single beer each night. I laughed and, remembering that he had quit smoking, suggested that he just smoke one cigarette a day. He immediately protested, "There's no way I can do that! That's different."

"No, it's not, Pop. It's exactly the same thing. Beer is just as addictive for me as cigarettes are for you."

As a result of my sobriety, my relationship with Mom and Pop has changed radically. I used to drink at least four beers before seeing them when they came to town. We just couldn't get along. I was extremely impatient with them, ready to pounce on the smallest disagreement. I always focused on what was wrong with them, what they needed to change, never examining my role, my side of the street, my responsibilities. As a result, visits would inevitably evolve into angry verbal jousts, which left everyone frustrated and upset.

Visiting my parents now is easy. I don't pick fights anymore, nor do I try to change them. I no longer need to feel superior, to be right and make them wrong. Instead, I concentrate on their good qualities and am able to appreciate them as parents and as people, warts and all.

Pat, my office manager and friend for many years, also initially could not understand why I considered myself an alcoholic. But after a year of my sobriety, she took me aside and said, "Bert, I hope you continue to leave alcohol alone."

"Why, Pat?"

"Well, don't be offended"—she laughed—"but you used to have severe mood swings at the office."

"What kind of mood swings?"

"Well, you used to get real irritable at times. I always thought it was a natural part of your personality that was triggered by work pressure or by the stress of trial preparation. I had no idea it had anything to do with alcohol. And I'm not saying you're perfect now, so don't get a big head, but you've really changed."

*A sporadically explosive personality is one of the hallmarks of some abnormal drinkers.* That character trait is most evident on Mondays, which is ordinarily the most difficult time for a functioning alcoholic—physically, emotionally, and mentally—following a weekend of excessive drinking.

Pat's observation gave me insight into my violent and aggressive behavior as a soccer player that had been "out of character," yet had repeated itself with regularity during weekend soccer matches. I was a wild man—a former enforcer from the rugby fields—who loved to run over opposing soccer players, particularly the quick and temperamental strikers, and send them flying through the air with arms and legs flailing. Irrational anger of unknown origin would boil over, as an otherwise gentle man gained a well-deserved reputation as a brute of a player.

It wasn't until I became sober and daily resolved the normal conflicts and stresses of life, without suppressing them temporarily with alcohol, that I realized a true sense of peace. At that point, the occasional bouts of senseless, displaced anger simply disappeared.

The change in my personality became most evident when I was walking across a hotel lobby recently in Alexandria, Virginia, and heard a woman's voice call out, "Bert Pluymen, is that you?" I turned and saw a black woman I did not recognize but whose voice sure matched that of Sallye Taylor, a spellbinding minister who could preach up a desert rainstorm.

"Sallye, is that you?"

"Yeah, darlin', it's me. How on earth have you been?"

We hugged and talked, and in the process forgave each other for some old misunderstandings that had occurred while I was a board member at her church. We had always cared deeply about each other, but a mutual failure to communicate had caused us to grow apart. Sallye was now in Sacramento, California, and had her own ministry, which she affectionately called Soul Food Ministries. Knowing her, there were many people being fed with the love of God and much laughter.

After a few minutes of catching up, Sallye said, "Honey . . . what's happened to you?"

For a second, I was worried. "What do you mean?"

"Well, I just can't believe how mellow you've become."

And she was right. As she spoke, I could feel my mellowness permeating the space around us. I had not previously noticed a difference, in the same way we don't see a puppy growing every day around our feet. But after five years, the radical change from stressed professional to peace-filled person was obvious to Sallye, and now to me. *Being sober had brought the unexpected gift of serenity into my life.* And it is a gift promised to anyone who works a program of recovery.

Like everyone else, Sallye was surprised that I was in recovery, and like most, she was very supportive. But a few people were not. One of my drinking buddies insisted that I was not an alcoholic. "Hey, you don't drink that much," he protested. "You don't drink any more than I do."

I told him, "Look, all I know is that it is time for me to stop. I don't know how it is for you; I just know what it's like for me, and I believe I need to quit. Maybe I'm wrong, but I would rather be living a sober life by mistake than continue drinking by mistake."

# 9

## DON'T FEEL BAD

If you suffer severe hangovers more often than you'd like, follow these handy rules:

- Eat cheese or buttered bread before going out to coat your stomach.

- Don't drink alcohol with soft drinks containing sugar, because the sugar causes the hangover.

- Do not drink fruit juice with alcohol.

- Stay away from red wine with its heavy residue.

- Avoid wines containing sulfides because your hangover may be caused by an allergy to the chemicals.

- Don't mix wine, beer, or whiskey. Stay with one drink. Mixing them causes the hangover.

- Drink only clear whiskey or whiskey with water. Unadulterated alcohol will not cause a hangover. The additives do.

- Drink two large glasses of water with aspirin before sleeping because dehydration causes the hangover.

- Drink water in the middle of the night if you wake up.

- Eat while you drink.

- Drink only white wine.

- Drink only beer.

- Be sure to pace your drinking.

- If you've had too much to drink, put a finger down your throat and throw up so you'll feel better in the morning.

- If you are unfortunate enough to have the "dry heaves," sip a soft drink to settle your stomach.

- In the morning, sweat out the hangover with exercise or in a steam bath or sauna.

- When all else fails, have some "hair of the dog that bit you."

If much of this list rings familiar, *you are not a normal drinker.* Normal drinkers do not have these concerns, have no interest in them, and no reason to have contemplated them. Only an abnormal drinker would explore these issues.

# 10

## WIND CHIMES

◼

Time has borne out the wisdom and accuracy of my decision to stop. Life is so much easier now. But that did not happen instantly. Unfortunately, it takes a while before a fundamental change in behavior manifests itself as a joyous and carefree life. All those years of drinking crank up a giant wind machine, creating what a friend affectionately describes as a "shit storm" of problems. And the wind doesn't magically stop when the machine is turned off. It will continue to blow for a while. But as long as you stand still and resist turning the machine back on, the wind *will* blow out.

Making amends for past behavior facilitates the process. Once sober, it is amazing how clearly we can see our role in situations which, we were always convinced, were totally someone else's doing—marriages and relationships that failed through "no fault of our own," business partnerships and close friendships that were supposedly destroyed solely by the other person. *Humbly acknowledging our role and making amends where feasible causes magical changes.*

The Big Book describes the miracles that occur when we have come this far:

> If we are painstaking about this . . . we will be amazed before we are half way through. We are going to know a new freedom and a new happiness. We will not regret the past nor wish to shut the door on it. We will comprehend the word serenity and we will know peace. No matter how far down the scale we have gone, we will see how our experience can benefit others. That feeling

of uselessness and self-pity will disappear. We will lose interest in selfish things and gain interest in our fellows. Self-seeking will slip away. Our whole attitude and outlook upon life will change. Fear of people and of economic insecurity will leave us. We will intuitively know how to handle situations which used to baffle us. We will suddenly realize that God is doing for us what we could not do for ourselves.

Are these extravagant promises? We think not. They are being fulfilled among us—sometimes quickly, sometimes slowly. They will *always* materialize if we work for them.[1]

*When these are the results, why live any other way?*

The alternative is a continuing struggle with alcohol, the accompanying pain, and a prematurely aging face. In talking to women who look to be in their late thirties and are still drinking heavily, I have often been shocked when they reveal that they just turned twenty-eight or twenty-nine. It's amazing how much younger such a woman looks just six months into sobriety. The change is that dramatic.

And, contrary to popular belief, you don't have to give up fun activities and people. Once you are confident in your sobriety, you can party with normal drinkers. At parties or clubs, most people are so into themselves that they'll never notice you're not drinking alcohol. After a few dates, a woman will usually notice that I don't drink and ask if it bothers me that she does. It honestly does not. I can have just as much fun as she does while drinking diet Coke or tonic-and-lime. And why should she not drink socially and enjoy herself with me? I would no more ask her not to drink than ask her not to eat oysters or shrimp if I were allergic to shellfish.

From the beginning of my sobriety, I vowed that if remaining sober wasn't as much fun as drinking, I would start again. Since then, there's been no need to avoid boredom or to create artificial excitement with alcohol. In fact, life without drinking has been more thrilling, in large part because I experience *everything*—good and bad.

Like many people, by the time I got sober, I was sick of my job and wanted to walk out the door. A sponsor convinced me not to throw away years of education and work, but to first let go of it in my heart. "Once you do that," he said, "your days will lighten instantly and your income will increase inexplicably." He was right.

"What then?"

"Gradually pay off your credit cards, your car note, and all other debts, leaving only your house payment—and reduce that if you can. At that point, you will feel as if a great weight has been lifted from your shoulders, and you will be free for the first time in your life."

"I want that so badly."

"Believe me," he said. "I've just been through it, and there's no experience like doing what you choose every day."

"I've heard of people who wake up each morning excited about their work and who can't wait to get started. I want that in my life."

"Become *willing* to let go of where you are now," he said. "Finish your responsibilities. And when you're ready to leave, other doors will be open and waiting for you to walk through."

Even though I had a good business, I was almost bankrupt when I became sober, mainly from having made poor investment decisions. "Being 'broke' just means you have nothing," I told my friend. "I owe so much money that I'm way below broke." In fact, the debt service was so onerous that I had felt like a slave to my creditors the previous five years.

Being sober and having the support and wisdom of the program gave me the courage to look people in the face and tell them that I couldn't continue down this self-destructive path. "I'm sorry," I would say, "but I just can't do it anymore." Some were gracious, appreciative that I'd made my payments for so many years, and called it even with the return of their collateral. Others agreed to a note with an easier payment schedule. The last three creditors were insured against any loss, were unwilling to negotiate, and simply foreclosed. But it was *over.*

I had been treading water, wearing weights, but now I could make progress. Four years of gradually paying down on debt—and I was *free.*

Today I have to be the most blessed person on earth. It's been three years since I sold my law practice, and I love what I do— which is writing and speaking. I rent a house on the lake and have to avoid the deer driving home. Looking out the window, I can see my joyful German shepherd barking at the water and jumping unprovoked off the dock, like a five-year-old kid.

And I wasn't going to talk about this for fear that some people wouldn't relate. But it's been true for me—I net more money now than when I was working full time. And I don't even know how to explain that. It's never been anything I solicited. Nothing I sought out. I've simply been watchful for doors that open before me, which represent opportunity. With each one that appears, I research the situation thoroughly and trustingly act where appropriate.

The bottom line: I believe that as long as you and I add value to life, whether at work, at home, or for strangers, Spirit will take care of us. No truer words were ever spoken than "What goes around, comes around." Long ago, I stopped believing in hell after death, because the fire produced by my actions couldn't wait that long to singe my butt. And the same has been true for my piece of heaven.

Who would have ever thought I had to join a group of recovering alcoholics to find it? But I sure couldn't navigate my way here on my own.

# PART THREE

# PERSONAL & SCIENTIFIC SNAPSHOTS

The captivating stories ahead were spoken into my tape recorder and edited for clarity and concision. The alternating chapters of fascinating scientific information are a summary of the countless technical journal articles and books that I reviewed.

# 11

## WHO ARE THE ALCOHOLICS AMONG US?

◼

Amazingly, half of all alcohol is quaffed by just 10 percent of the drinking population.[1]

Who's consuming it?

Many of the tipplers are young, since the sixteen to twenty-five age group contains both the largest portion of drinkers and the greatest amount consumed per person. Most people slow their intake with age, and substantially so by their late twenties or early thirties. But those who maintain or increase their earlier level are eventually diagnosed with addiction. That is, unless they die first—which is likely and occurs fifteen years earlier than expected.

What is the leading cause of their death? *Heart disease.* That's how destructive alcohol is to this vital muscle.[2] And although people addicted to alcohol find it necessary to seek medical treatment more frequently than normal for a variety of diseases, few ever seek treatment for their primary medical disorder. Those who do generally wait until their early forties—after years of difficulties.[3]

In the U.S. alone, about 15 million people meet the medical criteria for alcohol abuse or dependence.[4]

Who are these men and women?

According to popular belief, an alcoholic is a man whose drinking is totally out of control.* He has difficulty walking and slurs

---

*The traditional perception of the alcoholic as male is so pervasive that most people have difficulty picturing what a female alcoholic would look like. Excessive drinking by women is encouraged and ignored by our patriarchal society, because it is advantageous to men. Historically, women were instilled with the positive values of spirituality and family. Now, through massive advertising campaigns, a whole generation of women has been taught that drinking and partying are the road to happiness. Many of the fascinating stories in this book are about women, and the chapter "Wake-up Call for Women" explores the special sensitivity of women's bodies to alcohol.

his words. He can't hold a job because he drinks in the morning and stays drunk most days. Everyone immediately recognizes him for what he is and avoids him. Often, he is homeless or supported by a sympathetic wife or relative. If he drives, he wrecks cars and is frequently arrested for DWI. . . .

Most people addicted to alcohol fit a radically different profile, however. In fact, these men and women would be greatly offended if called "alcoholic." They still hold good jobs or own successful businesses, are still married and living with their spouse and children, or are single, seemingly carefree, and desirable. In time, though, their inevitable downward spiral, if unchecked, will gradually cause these men and women to lose everything. Yet, because alcohol creates its own invisible fog that impedes judgment and blocks the ability to see, these drinkers remain oblivious to their plight.

The typical addict works in an office or blue-collar job and alternates periods of abstinence or light drinking with intervals of misuse.[5] From day to day, most have no trouble with their drinking.[6] In fact, in any given month *half* of all people addicted to alcohol are temporarily on the wagon.[7] Fully 70 percent of addicted men and women quit at some point for at least three months.[8]

Most become aware that they drink too much and begin drinking only intermittently. At times, they even stop completely, either to prove to themselves that they aren't alcoholic or because circumstances dictate that drinking would be unwise. Eventually, they return to drinking and the addiction resumes unabated.

Usually the first real sign of trouble occurs in the drinker's late twenties or early thirties with job difficulties, an accident, or more typically, the loss of a beloved spouse, girlfriend, or boyfriend. Ironically, the breakup is sometimes initiated by the alcoholic, whose flawed perception prevents the personal adjustments, unrelated to drinking, that are vital to maintaining the relationship. Ordinarily, the alcoholic receives support from drinking friends, partly because of personal loyalty, and partly because their own judgment is clouded as well. Still more support comes from pervasive advertising, which glorifies alcohol as a product that makes a person more sociable, more fun, more attractive, more successful. Although this broken love relationship may cause severe emotional pain to the alcoholic, and perhaps scar any children involved, often neither party recognizes the subversive role played by alcohol.

As time goes on, the alcoholic imperceptibly loses most friends who are not heavy drinkers and becomes more isolated. Although people continue to call, particularly if the abnormal drinker is still an attractive woman or man, real friendship is missing. Gradually, the growing relationship with beer or another favorite drink makes this his most important, stable, and constant companion. In other words, when it really gets down to it, he can give up any person in his life but would never dream of giving up his favorite drink. By this point, life without the pleasure of alcohol does not seem worth living.

From here on, the only question is the depth of the landing place.

When an addicted person seeks medical care, the doctor will usually be looking at a sober, well-groomed bachelor, family man, homemaker, or professional woman who complains of minor problems like difficulty in sleeping, sadness, stress, or interpersonal problems. In middle age, the medical complaint may be a major illness such as pneumonia, heart disease, or cancer. Typically, no complaint about alcohol will be voiced and no sign of withdrawal will be apparent. In fact, many people who have life-threatening medical problems caused by alcohol, and who may even die of an alcohol-precipitated condition, never display visible signs of physical withdrawal.[9]

Instead, most addicts have mild, occasional withdrawal symptoms, which may include sweating, a fast pulse, very low fever, irritability, mood swings, or hyperventilation. Sadness, anxiety, or other emotional complaints are common, occurring in three of four people, while nausea and vomiting have been experienced by as many as one in two.[10]

Physical withdrawal from alcohol begins within twelve hours, peaks by the second or third day, and is virtually gone by the fourth or fifth. However, some anxiety, ranging from restlessness and irritability to occasional panic, can last for up to a year,[11] and sleep disturbance may persist for several years.[12]

The number of people addicted to alcohol is increasing rapidly.

The risk of addiction is twice what it was less than a generation ago.[13] Young people in most countries are at greater risk than ever, primarily because of more permissive attitudes toward drinking.[14]

Men have always been at greater risk than women, but women's rates are escalating, with the current generation of middle-aged women having a risk factor similar to that of men in their fathers' generation.[15] With the past explosion of alcohol consumption among girls and college coeds, we are likely to see a spate of articles about women seeking recovery.

Some nationalities have comparatively high rates of addiction to alcohol. The French, the Irish, the Koreans, the Russians, and various Native American tribes are particularly susceptible to its dangerous charms. The Chinese and Japanese, meanwhile, have appeared almost immune to developing a dependency, at least until recently.

What accounts for alcohol addiction in some and not in others? Is it a function of inheritance, the influence of environment, or both?

After you've had a chance to hear Ashley's moving story, we'll return to these questions.

# 12

◪

As a teenager, I once went to a party and drank eleven drinks—
I know, because I wrote it down afterward. Then I had sex
with a boy in a field. We lived in the English countryside, and it
was the first time I had ever had sex.

My mother wasn't sure what I'd done, but she had a rough idea
when I came home with streaked makeup and mud all over my
clothes. This boy had taken my clothes off. I wanted him to—it
was something I really wanted to do. But my clothes were covered
in mud from being thrown somewhere in the passion.

Mother was hysterical. "How could you *do* this to us?" she
screamed. "How could you do this to *me?*"

I just sat there, thinking, *I haven't done anything to you! That's
not right, what you think about it.*

"You're not going out anymore, ever again!" she said. "And I'm
going to talk to this boy!"

Fortunately she didn't, and two weeks later, my father left
Mother for her best friend. After that, he was totally absent, and my
mother was so out of her mind that however I behaved was no
longer an issue. My ban was lifted, and I was free to go out and do
it again. And I did. I did it over and over and over. . . .

With hindsight from therapy, I've learned that I simply wanted
the physical contact and affection we need as human beings. At the
time, though, I just knew that if I drank a lot and you talked to me,
I had sex, and it felt good—part of it, anyway.

I kept looking at my mother and thinking, *Why did he leave
her? She's prettier than other women. She's nicer and kinder. She
does more for me and my sister than any of my friends' mothers*

*do. She rarely gets angry or shouts at anybody. She never tells my
dad what to do. Why has he left us? What's wrong with her? And,
ultimately, what's wrong with me?*

Although it began with my mother, he left me too, you know,
because he never bothered with any of us after that.


As soon as I could, I left home to become a flight attendant.
Suddenly I'd found a whole world of people having fun and being
happy. They were physically active, liked to do things, and wanted
to see the world. I was so happy to be away from home, because
although everything seemed normal, my mother was a heartbroken
woman.

I was based in Saudi Arabia where there was no alcohol, but we
made our own. You drink more when it's banned, and many in our
group drank excessively.

I went to the Middle East as a twenty-year-old lost child who
didn't feel grown up. Because we were so isolated, the culture I
grew up in was the airline world. When I was transferred to New
York after several years and flew all through Asia, I stayed in that
world. Most airline people would go home to their families and
friends. They'd step out of that world. I didn't.

And inside that world there's drinking and sex—and I had a
wonderful time. It's not like it sounds in that I wouldn't sleep
with just anybody, but I was happy for the first time and thoroughly enjoyed myself. I did drink a great deal, but it wasn't a
problem. The only time it ever occurred to me that something
might be wrong was that I would cry sometimes. Even when I was
truly happy, I would get drunk and cry and not know why, and
that puzzled me.

After moving to New York, I took a second job and exercised
harder than any of my friends. To work hard and to look good—
what else is there to life? I had never heard of anything else.

The things I knew worked in my world—work hard, exercise
hard, drink hard, fuck hard. And I did, and it worked.

But when I was twenty-six, I fell in love, and we both wanted to
marry. The relationship lasted only a year, though, and then went
wrong. I didn't understand why or how to mend it. It was broken.

"Never mind, it doesn't matter," I told myself. "I won't dwell on it. Let's not get upset over spilt milk. Let's get on with life."

But that was the turning point in my drinking—I went over the top. After that, on days off, I drank beer all day long, didn't eat much, and became very thin. I wouldn't sleep with anybody, but I would date two or three men in a night.

I once believed I never told lies, yet I would say to you, "Sure, I'd love to see you later! I'll be at the gym until eight, and then it'll take me an hour. I won't be free until about 9:30, if that's all right— maybe 10:00, to be on the safe side."

Then I'd go out with somebody else and tell him I had to be home early because I had something important to do in the morning. A couple of times I even dumped my ten o'clock date at 1:00 A.M. to go to a club with my girlfriends and meet someone else. I was pretty, and if a man I was dating took me to task, I'd think, *Screw you. I'll meet another guy tomorrow.*

Then I wondered why no one would take me seriously, why I couldn't seem to connect with anybody, and why I couldn't meet the right sort of man. It was insane. *I* was insane. "What am I doing wrong?" I'd fret. I'd try looking prettier, work out harder at the gym, and see more men.

I went out almost every single night of the week from age twenty-seven to thirty, because if I wasn't out, I thought I was a bloody loser. Then I felt bad because I didn't have anything else. "What's wrong with me?" I'd wonder. By now, there really was something wrong with me. By now, I drank way too much.

I had been living by my simple and rigid set of rules: Never lie and cheat in bed. Never ever date a man who is married or seeing somebody else. Never have a time in your life that's unaccountable. In other words, be productive every moment—and I considered being shitfaced productive. That was doing something. That was going out. That was being busy, which was in the rules—you have to be busy. I didn't even believe in God, but I thought He gave us something special, and if you dare not use that time productively, shame on you. Some of my girlfriends were very complacent about life, and I thought that was pitiful.

It's funny, I was always being so sophisticated—hanging out in the classiest nightclubs, wearing exquisite clothes. I earned good money and could shop anyplace. But my therapist once told me, "Well, it doesn't sound very sophisticated to me if you're always blind drunk, picking up handsome strangers." It had never occurred to me that I wasn't elegant.

I thought being refined was drinking champagne, wearing fancy clothes, being in the right club, and picking up gorgeous professional men who occasionally gave me cocaine. It sounds crazy, but it felt very dignified. I didn't feel I had a problem doing coke for a time. If you had a problem with coke, you'd be a drug addict, wouldn't you?

In doing all this, I never got arrested. I didn't have to drive because I lived in New York, where nobody has a car. Whether I would have if circumstances were different, I don't know. Plus I'm a woman. It's very easy to talk your way out of things.

Then I met a man who just came from another planet. I had never met anyone like him in my life. He took me to dinner and to my home. "I had a really nice time," he said. "Good night."

I was absolutely baffled!

"No big deal," I decided, then put my coat back on and went out again. It was eleven o'clock at night, so I went to a party and got drunk.

A couple of days later I ran into him, and we went out again. He would touch me, but not sexually, and I had never had or done that before. It fascinated me, and it felt really nice. He was an alcoholic in recovery, and he was a real friend to me. I needed practical help because I was starting my own import business, and he was in the same trade.

He was calm and kind. He had what I know today to be "boundaries." He'd assist me to a point and then he'd say, "It's up to you now." Or, "I can't do any more, I'm sorry."

He would tell me that he liked being with me and looked forward to seeing me, but he still wasn't pushing me for sex. He would drop me off and not come into my apartment. I was intrigued and baffled. He would stand there and I would think, *Do something!* I was raring to go—and nothing!

He was all those things, and then he was something else as well: He was the father of a two-year-old girl to whom he was absolutely devoted. She lived half the time with him, and he spent a lot of time with her. It dawned on me that that existed. I'd had no idea that fathers paid attention to their daughters.

He cared about her, and he went out of his way to do things for her. I was just awestruck by that. And I got into a terrible state about it. My whole world was . . . *cracking*. I thought I was starting to go mad because I was so emotional. It was unusual for me to lose my temper and feel depressed, but stuff was coming out in me, and I didn't know where it was coming from. *Who's doing this crying? Who in me said that? Why? Where did that anger come from?* It was just awful. I couldn't keep it down anymore.

Meantime, I was drinking, drinking, drinking. I had my way of living and the things I did and who I was and how I behaved and the way I felt and thought—created by circumstance, genetics, personality, and character—and all that was dying. I was discovering I hadn't got all the rules right.

But I don't see alcohol being responsible for the way I lived. Not at all. I see them being two parallel things. I made good choices and terrible choices based upon my view of life. And I drank, and just drank more.

Alcohol's a drug, and I became addicted to it. It's actually as simple as that.

The effect of the drinking was that it put an invisible barrier between me and the rest of the world. I didn't know it was there, and it prevented me from seeing and feeling.


I stumbled across a book while on a business trip to Indonesia. It kept me awake all night, and I cried the whole way through. The book was word for word about me. I kept closing it and staring at the cover, which said *Adult Children of Alcoholics,* and it continually referred to "dysfunction" and "unhealthy family dynamics."

Although my parents didn't drink much—they were sensible—everything else in that book went on in our house. In the introduction, it says something like, "We believe that this concept applies to children who grew up in homes of trauma."

I was so sure I was normal, but the book and my emotional outbursts were telling me I wasn't. So I drank and drank in the Orient, and on coming back to New York, I thought, *I've got to act.*

*Something's happening to me. I don't know what it is, but it's got something to do with my dysfunctional family background. I know what—I'll go to Al-Anon.\**

I stopped drinking while going to Al-Anon because otherwise I'd feel like a hypocrite. I wasn't an alcoholic, I was sure. And there was no *way* I was going to AA. But something was wrong, and here was a group offering help in relationship dynamics. I didn't know if the two were going to connect, but I was thinking fast enough to try something.

Going there helped me a great deal. They employed a whole language I'd never heard—talking about how you feel. I didn't understand it because how do you tell someone how you feel if you don't really know? I had no clue.

But my relationships with bank tellers, postal workers, and others was not the best. For example, I would park my business van in the street and a policeman would say, "Now, lady, you can't park there."

"What the fuck do you mean, I can't park here?" I'd protest. "Why can't I park here?" I never knew what was setting me off, but I was so angry much of the time.

Al-Anon helped me incredibly over a couple of months. But I was still somewhat sad, bewildered, and confused, not able to understand why somebody who worked so hard at everything was struggling. I didn't even drink anymore, so what was I doing wrong?

*Well, I don't know what the answer is,* I thought, *but this isn't it. So I'm gonna drink.*

I did, though not as much as before. Yet I still felt uncomfortable while staying with a nondrinking girlfriend in California, and for the first time in my life, I hid what I drank. Everybody I knew drank, and I'd never noticed my drinking until I lived with her.

On the way home from work, I would stop at a deli and drink three beers before going to the house. And then she'd see me drink another three or four. Even then, she commented once or twice, "You shouldn't have that wine with lunch. You're going to be sleepy

---

*An Al-Anon Family Group is a fellowship of friends and relatives of alcoholics who share their experience, strength, and hope in order to solve their mutual problems. They believe alcohol addiction is a family disorder and that changed attitudes can assist recovery.

this afternoon." But I wanted wine when we'd have lunch together, because no enjoyable occasion was complete without a drink.

For several months, I was very conscious of how much I drank. Then I went to the hairdresser one morning, and she absolutely ruined my hair. I came out of the salon at 11:00, saw a liquor store across the street, and bought a half-pint of vodka. I hailed a cab, and told the driver to take me to a trade show. En route, I drank some of the vodka and felt so good that I thought, *This is how I want to live! The hairdresser can do whatever she wants to my hair. It doesn't matter.*

While attending the show, I felt numb. But I had been like that for a long time. Here was me, and there was the world, and the gap is where the alcohol was. And I loved feeling numb. So I spent the entire day there, sipping an occasional soft drink and vodka, and then met friends at five o'clock in a bar. I drank the whole day, feeling good, not drunk at all.

But the next morning, I thought, *My, God, how can I go through life if I can't visit the hairdresser without needing to drink because she screws up my hair? Something's* very *wrong.*


I went to an AA meeting that same day—I didn't want to wait.

"If you want what we've got," they kept saying, "and you'll go to any lengths to get it, then you'll have to take certain steps." And they had something I wanted. They were peaceful, and I had a merry-go-round in my head. I was very troubled and couldn't understand why I wasn't happy.

I was incredibly lucky and blessed. I'd bought a house when I was twenty-two. By the time I was twenty-six, I'd been most of the way around the world. Most people in rural England never get those opportunities.

I flew to Saint-Tropez, Cairo, Athens, Nairobi, New Delhi, Tokyo, Hong Kong, Bangkok . . . Had vacations in Australia and Acapulco . . . Stayed at the most exclusive hotels with airline discounts . . . How could you fail to be happy?

There was a period where good things happened all the time, and I was very happy. So I drank because I was so happy. But when bad things happened, such as a breakup, I drank over those, too. Finally, I drank in response to everything.

To be totally honest about it, I knew I drank too much and couldn't live like that anymore. I didn't go to AA because I was an alcoholic, I went because I wanted to stop drinking. And when I got there, I realized some of them had many other wonderful things, and I wanted what they had. I hadn't been participating in life and thought I was.

How do you know you drink too much? I thought everybody did like I did. You have no other reference. I had no idea it wasn't normal to throw up. I had no idea it wasn't normal to sleep with a man you didn't know. And I'm not being facetious. How would I know?

Especially when your attractive girlfriends are doing the same thing. They weren't *all* doing it, but the ones who weren't never said they went home at the end of a date. And you know what? I had the funniest stories. My girlfriends would scramble to hear about my latest conquest, laughing because I'd get myself into the most amazing scrapes. And I would entertain them, because I thought their lives were so boring.

My drinking pattern became clear in my mind because of a sponsor who had only a year of sobriety when I was counting days. She couldn't throw much sober information my way, but she listened to me and it worked. She had me write out twenty occasions that came to mind where I got really drunk. I don't think she really knew what she was doing, but I was shocked when I told her about them. After I got to about the fourth or fifth one, I said, "This is stupid! You don't really want to hear any more, and I don't want to tell you. Ultimately, they're all the same."

Most ended with me either coming home and throwing up or sleeping with somebody I didn't know. One of the worst times, I was drunk on a ski holiday, became furious at my boyfriend, and literally attacked him.

I kept that handwritten list from early sobriety, and when I read it today, I think, *No wonder I felt so unfulfilled. No wonder I felt terrible and despairing. No wonder I thought I was dying inside.*

At first, I didn't share at meetings. I was there to listen. Although I didn't fully comprehend what I was listening to, I wasn't drinking and it felt good. And that was amazing! That was all I needed, and it was enough.

I heard people talk about "faith" and "trust" and about "live-and-let-live." That was new to me—to let go of control.

After several months of feeling good, though, I started becoming agitated and angry. What I couldn't understand more than anything was how I had lost my sense of judgment, being unable to gauge anything or anybody. I couldn't trust myself to do the right thing. Although I was convinced I was an adult, I was a child in many ways. So I stayed close to the meetings and threw myself into work.

After three months at meetings, I also began to hear other things. I began to hear people who were mentally ill. I began to hear people I didn't like. I began to hear talk about lying and cheating, which I had never, ever done.

I heard incredibly selfish people—all they ever talked about was themselves. And they said peculiar things, like, "Well, it's my sister's wedding and everybody in my family wants me to be there, but I can't be around alcohol right now, so I'm not going." And then everyone would clap.

*What a fucking selfish bastard!* I thought. *Your sister is getting married once in a lifetime, costing your family thousands of dollars, and all you've got to do is go for a couple of hours, and you're so wrapped up in your own goddamn problems, you can't do that for somebody else. That's sick!*

I didn't want to do it anymore, but I didn't want to drink either. And I heard and saw genuinely happy people, so I kept going. By my second anniversary, it dawned on me that I had no friends in the program, because people talked about their wonderful relationships and it used to piss me off.

They would say, "Susan helped me so much! Remember when I used to call and cry, Susan?"

I had purposely made no friends in my early meetings. I knew that I needed to be honest in order to recover. But I had to feel safe and run no risk of rejection. And if you didn't know me, you couldn't reject me. So I just wouldn't connect with anybody. And they were all losers anyway—they all had a drinking problem.

They said, "If you don't want to drink, you have to come to the meetings. And the meetings consist of people being honest, talking about how they feel and what's going on."

So I said, "OK, if that's what a meeting is, I'll do that. But I don't want to know you. You're just at the meeting. I'm very good at being alone and have spent my whole life needing no one. I worked real hard at that, and I'm not giving it up now."

But after two years, I yearned for friendship and began attending the same meeting regularly, making it my home group. I was amazed at how hard it was for me. I thought that since I had gone to Saudi Arabia alone at twenty and survived, that since I came to New York at twenty-four and established my own business and thrived, that I could do anything. I didn't need *anybody.* I didn't want people to see me cry, and I didn't need sympathy or help.

After a relationship ended, I went into therapy, and it was a huge help. AA had stopped me from drinking. And until I stopped, I was at a dead end—as long as I drink, I am finished. As long as I don't, I can do anything. But as soon as I stopped, I'd expected hurting would go away, and when it didn't, I sought help.

I could never have succeeded in therapy without the program because I didn't know what honesty was and couldn't have opened up. I wouldn't have known how. AA taught me to be aware of when I'm lying—not to you, but to *me.*

I discovered how hurt I was about my father's behavior. As difficult as it was to walk away from a therapy session totally drained, the following day I felt lighter. And the next time something didn't go my way, I wouldn't lose my temper. In retrospect, recovery has been slow paced, but I'm very much aware of how I behave now, and what I do and why.

My life at thirty-three is rather ordinary compared to the way it was. I don't travel to the same grand places or wear the glamorous clothes, and I definitely don't receive the kind of attention I got ten years ago. But I'm incredibly grateful for everything I have. Didn't even know the meaning of the word five years ago. I have everything I need. I used to hear people say that and think, *What a crock! Who wants everything they* need? *What about what I* want?"

I still get emotional. Just three weeks ago, something happened that hurt much more than I thought it would. I hung on, close to tears, until I came home, then literally slid down the wall, sitting with my knees under my chin, crying. But it was sadness, not despair. It wasn't bottomless and I knew I was going to be OK. In a weird way, it almost felt good.

Now I have peace of mind. I'm able to face a confusing situation and find the answer within myself. Before, I would find a dozen people to ask, "What do you think? Should I? Shouldn't I?" Now I trust my instincts more. I had annihilated them, but they're coming back—so I listen to my heart more than my head, and that's a big one for me.

Today I understand the man who doesn't go to his sister's wedding in early sobriety because it's a life-or-death struggle, and that's why some people must go to incredible lengths to stay sober.

Assisting other women is one of the biggest thrills of all. After becoming reasonably proficient at taking care of yourself, which normally takes a few years, then you're able to be there for somebody else. I don't matter so much. I can forget about myself and say, "Well, this isn't about me. She *needs* you." You can work through your challenge with alcohol, but that's not the point. It's not just about learning to take care of yourself and stopping there.

As far as the losers go, well, they're not drinking, are they? My idea of a loser was someone who didn't dress well or eat in the right restaurants. Now a loser is anyone who's arrogant or selfish.

Now I understand what life can be like when you're human, when you actually allow yourself to be emotionally present. Probably the biggest one of all is to be a bit vulnerable. And I look at what I did before and realize, "I was living on a planet *so* far away from this one."

# 13

## GRANDPA MADE ME

◪

If I hadn't inherited my alcoholism,
my family would have left me nothing.

—anonymous

Most of us have always thought that personal choice, influenced by environment, was the sole cause of dependency on alcohol—and that the remedy lies in an exercise of willpower. One professor had a simple solution:

> It is notable that many persons who live sedentary lives are vulnerable to alcoholism. Writers, actors and actresses, lawyers, politicians, and others who often are inactive physically are vulnerable, particularly when they also are affluent and can afford to loaf—and drink. Many of these individuals would lose their vulnerability if they routinely engaged in physical exercise, thus strengthening their internal environments.[1]

But tell that to the mice whose ancestry meant they were born with a natural preference for alcohol over water! In the 1950s, Dr. Leonora Mirone, associate professor of nutrition research at the University of Georgia, bred just such a strain.[2] Down in Santiago, meanwhile, Dr. Jorge Mardones, a nutritionist at the University of Chile, found that rats preferred alcohol if their ancestors had chosen the devil's brew before them.[3] The genetics were so predictable that crossbreeding drunkards and teetotalers resulted in rodent offspring that drank modestly.[4]

Yet the question remained: Can humans inherit a genetic preference for alcohol, as mice and rats can?

That's not easy to answer anecdotally, because, as one wag notes, "No one wrote in the family Bible that Aunt Jennie was a lush."

What's needed is a method for tracking alcohol-preferring humans and their progeny.

## Adoption Studies

Scientists exploring a potential genetic basis of alcoholism prefer to study adopted children. That way, any inherited tendency can be isolated from the environmental influence of an alcoholic home. But studying adopted children often presents a problem in determining parentage. And even when ancestry is correctly ascertained, there is the need to detect alcoholism in the family. For researchers in most nations, these two hurdles are formidable.

Luckily, the Scandinavian countries have kept excellent birth and alcoholism records, whose study has been enlightening. In tracking children who were adopted soon after birth, it was discovered that babies of an alcoholic father, adopted by nonalcoholic parents, are nearly *four* times more likely to become alcoholic than babies of normal parents.[5]

And here's an equally interesting finding: Babies who had normal parents, but were adopted by an alcoholic stepfather, are at no greater risk of becoming alcoholic than the general population.[6]

Clearly, genetics does influence the tendency to become alcoholic.

One Swedish study tracked all babies born out of wedlock between 1930 and 1949 who were adopted by nonrelatives. These babies were separated from their parents at the average age of four months and were adopted by the median age of eight months. The rate of alcohol addiction for children of a known alcoholic parent was up to 3.5 times greater than normal.[7]

A Danish study analyzed babies from similar backgrounds who had been separated by age six weeks and adopted into comparable homes. By age twenty-nine, those born to alcoholic parents had an addiction rate of 20 percent compared to 5 percent with normal parents.[8] That's four times greater than normal.

Since addiction often does not become apparent until drinkers reach their thirties, a much higher rate would be expected for both groups after age twenty-nine. True to form, when two student groups from Boston, Massachusetts, were tracked through age fifty-five and sixty, the lifetime rate of alcohol addiction for normal offspring was 9–10 percent as compared to a 26–34 percent rate for students with several alcohol-abusing relatives.[9]

## How Many Times Have You Been Divorced?

The child of an alcoholic is not only *four* times as likely to become addicted to alcohol, but is also *three* times more likely to have been divorced.[10]

## He's Got Nothing to Do with Me

Persons with an alcoholic parent often don't recover without the severest symptoms because of their subconscious refusal to admit they are like their mother or father.[11]

## Broken Homes and Poverty

What about the influence of broken homes or poor families? A forty-year study of middle school students showed that kids from *strong* homes with an alcoholic parent became alcohol-dependent at a rate of 27 percent compared to just 5 percent of kids from broken homes with no alcoholic parent.[12]

In other words, if you come from an unstable or poor family, your chances of becoming alcoholic are increased only if the instability or poverty was caused by the presence of an alcoholic parent.[13]

## When the Family Tree House Is a Tavern

A higher addiction rate to alcohol is predictable not just from parentage, but also from the number of other alcoholic ancestors in the family tree. A summary of numerous studies conducted over the last eighty years concludes that at least 25 percent of the close relatives of alcoholics will become addicted.[14] And the closer the connection, the greater the rate. For instance, practically one out of every three known alcoholics has at least one addicted parent.[15]

## Our Family's Had Enough to Drink

Environment also influences addiction. For example, children of an addicted parent often choose not to drink at all because of their negative experiences at home.[16]

## Out of Sight, Out of Mind

Children who have addicted ancestors other than their parents, however, show only an increase in addiction with no accompanying rise in abstinence.[17] In other words, they are exposed to the genetic vulnerability, but haven't been close enough to the practicing alcoholics in the family to have sworn off alcohol.

## Twin Studies

One way to determine genetic influence is to study people with the greatest similarity: twins. Fraternal twins are born from two eggs and share 50 percent of their genes. They have no more similarity than ordinary brothers and sisters; they are simply born at the same time. Identical twins, however, are born from a single egg and share 100 percent of their genes. If one twin is addicted to alcohol, does the rate of addiction for the other twin vary depending on whether they share 50 percent or 100 percent of their genes?

Most definitely.

A Swedish study of 174 twin pairs showed a 28 percent addiction rate for fraternal twins, and a predictable doubling of the rate to 54 percent for identical twins.[18] Doubling your genetic resemblance may not just double your pleasure and fun.

## Sorry, Alcohol Is No Excuse for Your Personality

Some studies claim to detect inherent personality traits in people addicted to alcohol. These investigations typically scrutinize only individuals who have recently presented themselves at treatment centers or hospitals. Such an approach fails to exclude traits caused by excessive drinking.

However, Dr. George Vaillant, director of the Study of Adult Development at Harvard University, used a unique and laborious approach. He followed two large groups of students into their sixties to see which of them developed an addiction to alcohol.

Contrary to conventional wisdom, he found that adults who became addicted had *not* been insecure or psychologically burdened children, who later compensated for their subconscious defects by drinking. In fact, he found they differed little from normal children. If anything, they exhibited *greater* self-confidence and fewer anxieties! In short, they were well-adapted children, and any deficit in their coping skills as adults stemmed from their drinking.[19]

Sometimes, people in recovery refer to a "typical character trait" that's part of their addiction. It might be low self-esteem, depression, irritability, anxiety, anger, helplessness, compulsiveness, selfishness, arrogance, or even occasional megalomania. Research shows, however, that these are *temporary conditions caused by drinking,* not innate or permanent character traits.[20]

There's only one common personality characteristic among recovering alcoholics—we all drank too much.

## Why Couldn't I Have Inherited a
## High Tolerance for Money Instead?

"Tolerance" for alcohol means that more is needed to have the same effect. Tolerance occurs fairly quickly in a regular drinker, but is it a trait that can be inherited?

In searching for an answer, scientists tested the balancing ability on a beam of three special breeds of mice, one alcohol-preferring, the other two normal. They empirically proved what Grandma could have told us: a higher dosage of alcohol was necessary to disturb the balance of the alcohol-preferring mice than the normal water drinkers.[21]

This decreased reaction to the effect of alcohol may be inherited in humans as well. In laboratory tests, sons of alcoholic fathers describe significantly fewer feelings of intoxication than young men with normal dads, despite having identical blood-alcohol levels.[22]

But what difference does it make that some young people appear to have a higher tolerance for alcohol?

Researchers decided to follow a group of young men who at age twenty had shown a low level of response to alcohol. Some had fathers who were alcoholic; others didn't. By age thirty, these young men had a 43 percent chance of becoming alcoholic, as compared to just 11 percent of men who had earlier shown a high level of response to alcohol.[23] In other words, any twenty-year-old who has a high tolerance for alcohol is four times more likely to become alcoholic by age thirty, regardless of whether there is any family history of alcoholism.

Clearly, some young people are physically impeded from realizing the effects of their drinking. Whereas normal drinkers who overindulge get warning signals, such as dizziness or nausea, persons with a high tolerance for alcohol will often be oblivious under the same conditions.

This "tends to encourage them to 'take a chance' with heavier drinking, opening the way to alcohol abuse," according to one scientist. In fact, the above experiments "helped to correct the long-held myth that 'he-men' and strong-willed women can 'hold their liquor.' On the contrary, the findings suggested that people who don't 'get drunk' easily in the beginning may be the very ones who are at gravest risk of becoming alcoholics."[24]

Or, as Harvard's George Vaillant put it: "Contrary to the assertion that alcoholics are sensitive or 'allergic' to alcohol, the truth may be that . . . the person genetically at risk for alcoholism may be the individual with a 'hollow leg': the one who can drink his friends under the table without vomiting, losing his coordination, or suffering a hangover the next morning."[25]

## I Knew I Peaked Too Soon

In searching for physical differences between young people that might indicate which of them are vulnerable to alcohol addiction, scientists discovered a brain-wave peak—dubbed the "P300 peak"—which occurs while the brain is processing information. They found that boys from genetically high-risk families have a significantly lower P300 peak than kids who are at low risk for alcoholism.

Here's how it works:

As part of a fun experiment, children are asked to respond to a series of sounds. They push a button on the left in response to a high tone and one on the right for a low tone. While the brain is processing this flow of information and discriminating between high and low, a computer maps the electrophysiologic activity of the brain, using a series of electrodes attached to the skull. Differences in brain-wave activity can now be compared, particularly the maximum height of the P300 wave, which occurs each time a child's brain processes a new piece of sound information.

From tests involving a variety of children, we now know that many *nondrinking* young sons of alcoholics naturally exhibit a decreased P300 amplitude.[26] Though the jury is still out on young daughters of alcoholic fathers, girls with an alcoholic mother display a significantly lower P300,[27] as do adult women alcoholics in general.[28]

It is too early to say that a low P300 peak represents an electrophysiological marker in the brain for kids susceptible to alcohol addiction, or to conclude that it represents a genetic predecessor of alcohol abuse, but it certainly is one sign that *inherited differences relevant to alcohol are located in the brain.*

## Conclusion

Animal breeding, adoption studies, twin comparisons, and various tests on young persons all point to this: the tendency toward addiction, *for some people,* is a genetic time bomb just waiting to explode.

# 14

## MICHAEL

■

Mom left my twin brother and me when we were two. At the time she and Dad divorced, he was already a full-fledged alcoholic, and she left us with him. Dad was a telephone man—the nicest guy in the world until he got six beers in him. Then his moods would swing wildly from depression to fits and rages. I don't remember much about living with him, but I woke up many times as a young child to find him gone. My brother and I always took care of ourselves—made our own lunches, did our own clothes . . .

When Mom came back into our lives when I was eight, she took us to live on a farm. She had a new husband, and he physically abused my brother and me for several years. When I was fourteen, Mom finally divorced him, too. Back we went to the city.

As you can imagine, I was full of anger and would fight somebody for just looking at me wrong. Then I got introduced to marijuana and alcohol, and that was it—most of the pain and anger was gone.

After getting away from our stepfather, my brother and I vowed that no one would ever control our lives again. As farm children we had always worked after school, clearing land, hauling posts, feeding animals. So after we moved, we got jobs and supported ourselves. We delivered newspapers all through high school and worked at McDonald's in the evening.

By this time, Mom knew she couldn't handle us, period. She had married again, and I got in a fight with my new stepfather and pulled a knife on him. Somehow the next day we were back at

Dad's house. And that's the way it went. I've had four stepfathers and three stepmothers—no direction in my life.


By the time I was in high school, Dad was such a drunk that, for two years, he was hardly ever home, spending most of his time in jails and state hospitals. My brother and I never questioned what to do. We just got up, went to school, worked, came home—and partied.

There was absolutely no adult supervision, nor could anyone control us. Our house became the party house. All my friends would come over because Dad wasn't there. Always pot coming in. If not from me, then from someone else. And we constantly had beer. Dad even bought it at times because he knew he couldn't stop us and figured it was better for him to buy it than someone else.

Drinking was this huge escape. "Let's party, man! Let's have a good time!" That was my purpose in life. Drinking was a personal declaration: *"This* is the good life! We've made it through the bad times. Now it's time to relax and celebrate!"

Although I was easygoing and people liked to party with me, there were times when I ended up in fights. I don't know if it had anything to do with me. Stupid episodes where somebody would come up and start a fight for no apparent reason. And something inside of me would just explode. But when that happened, I was always drunk. It never happened sober.

I drank mainly on weekends and at parties, but once I got off to being stoned, I smoked every day. I would do a bowl in the morning before school, and we'd get stoned at lunch. After school we had to have beer, and beer and pot make a nice mixture. I didn't really want pot without a couple of beers, and I didn't want beer without some pot to go with it. Not surprisingly, I failed every class my freshman year and took extra classes the last three years just to graduate on time.

I know I'm not dumb because I never took books home and still passed. I'd sleep through class from partying, then stay up all night before a test and scrape by. My teachers were so pissed because it was such a waste. I'm not proud of it now because I want to be a writer and don't know a thing about history or science.

———

Dad got sober and joined AA when I was twenty-one, and he wanted to introduce me to the program. My girlfriend and I were having problems, and I was always telling him what was going on. And he would say, "Well, maybe you should check out a meeting." That's all. He would never push.

Just to shut him up, one time I said, "All right, Dad, we'll go to a meeting." I was twenty-two and had been drinking since I was thirteen. We went to a young persons' group, and I stood under a stupid-ass air conditioner and didn't listen to a word anybody said. I was already stoned—I had to get stoned before going—and I didn't go back for a long time.

A year later, my girlfriend left me, and I was lonely. I had never in my life gone without a girlfriend for more than a week. When you're younger, it's much easier to meet girls. Nobody really cares about getting to know one another—they just want to jump right into a relationship. And it wasn't happening anymore. I didn't know why, but I knew it had something to do with me. So I went to a meeting on my own.

I didn't want to quit drinking. What I really wanted was to get sober so I could figure out what was wrong with me, then go back out, find me a girl, and start drinking again. I stayed sober two months, and drank as soon as my old girlfriend and I made up. *All right, I got her back,* I thought. *Party time!*

My girlfriend never said my drinking or pot smoking bothered her. But sometimes I would say, "I need to stop drinking."

"You're right," she would say. "You do." But I wasn't ready.

I never thought of myself as anything other than a normal drinker until I was twenty-four, when I realized that I drank every single day, and had for as long as I could remember. But it wasn't a problem. A problem drinker is somebody who drinks so much that it affects their job. That had never been true for me. The responsibility of work had been ingrained in me since childhood, and even with all the drinking and dope smoking, I always arrived early. No matter how late I stayed up, no matter how wasted I'd been, I always got there. Because if I didn't pay my bills, nobody would.

The recognition that my drinking was excessive didn't motivate me to do anything about it. It was only when I tried to be in a serious loving relationship that I realized that my pot and alcohol were more important. My girlfriend and I argued and fought all the time. And every time she left me, the drinking would get worse. And that's when I would think about it. Alone, I would think, *Man, I'm fucked up. I'm crazy in the head.*

Normally, my drinking was under control. It was mostly a six-pack a day and a joint. Just high maintenance. But I *could* drink that much. I never had a blackout, although I got sick sometimes when I drank too much. But I could drive, no problem at all. I could work. I functioned great. No matter how much alcohol I put in my body, I kept going. All I needed was a joint and a six-pack. After that, I was fine.

It was only when my relationship started going downhill that I began to think maybe I had a problem. By then Dad had already been sober for two or three years. I'd question my drinking and go to AA meetings, but I didn't like it. They didn't understand that I'd made it through a shithole of an adolescence with nine parents. I had worked and been responsible since I was eight, and I'd never had any fun. My first stepmother had thrown away all my toys when I was six. I was determined to make up for every bit of lost fun by drinking and smoking.

What I wanted most was just to be loved, but I didn't know how. And when I started listening to people in AA, I began to realize that you could learn those things. But for years, I found it very hard to stay sober.


After my girlfriend and I had been reconciled for a while, I decided to tell her that I had slept with a couple of other girls while we were apart. That secret had been eating at me, and I wanted to get it off my chest. So I decided to tell her. And she dumped me.

Two days later, I found out my best friend, who had been HIV positive, had developed full-blown AIDS. Knowing that he was in the hospital, dying, and that I had to go see him, I lost it—crying and drinking, and beating on the walls. When I did see him, he looked awful. My insides were out of control, and I knew I needed help. Standing outside the hospital that night, I took a leak on the front lawn and thought about throwing a rock through the plate glass window so they would come and arrest me and I could get sober. But I didn't have the guts. Instead, I went home, called a friend I'd made at AA, and got sober for the longest time ever— almost four months to the day my best friend died.

Then an incredible thing happened. I got a job offer to work as a production assistant in the film industry in Utah. All my life I had wanted to be in the movie business as a writer or actor. Now here I was, living in the mainstream of the industry. And it was fantastic. Most people have a hard time getting and keeping film work, but I worked two years straight, going from one production to the next. Every time a show would end, I'd freak and go, "Oh, man, am I going to work on another movie?" A week later there would be another kick-ass show to work on. It was a dream come true.

In Utah, with four months' sobriety, I felt pretty good about my control over drinking. I even went to a couple of meetings. But it was so different from my home group. These were all hard-core drunks, Big Book thumpers, and people who were like eighty years old. There was nobody my age, and, boy, did I feel out of place. Plus I was working sixteen- to eighteen-hour days.

Then one night we were working on the side of a mountain, and there was pizza and beer. Nothing else to drink. Absolutely nothing. And I was starving. So I had three pieces of hot pizza . . . mouth burning . . . thirsty . . . and I said, "Fuck it . . . give me a beer." By the time I got home at two in the morning, I was so angry because I'd had five beers—and wanted more. I had been in Utah all of three weeks.

The next two years, no matter how many hours I worked, I still needed three or four beers to get to sleep, and the usual joint to start me off in the mornings. When you work on movies, you can work eighteen to twenty hours a day, go home, sleep three hours, come back, and go for more than a week straight. And still, no matter what, I always had to get drunk and stoned, because that was my party time. That was when I got to sit back and relax and say, "Look, man, I did it! Look where I'm at. I'm so cool!"

I had everything in life going for me—the best job . . . money for the first time in my life . . . my bills paid . . . lots of travel. I still didn't have a great relationship, but everything else was wonderful. I thought about it often before it dawned on me, "You know, man, this is not making me happy. I don't care how many famous people I meet, this is not what I want to be doing." Here I had the chance to do what I always wanted, and I wasn't happy doing it.

It wasn't until all these exterior things were going so well and I *still* couldn't be happy that I realized, "You know, it's the drinking. It's the damn drinking."

I had already seen Dad be sober for seven years. I had seen others get sober, and a number of people on the set didn't drink. I had worked on one production around a famous author, who's my idol, and I got the impression he was sober. He never told me so, but there were enough things we talked about, little hints, that made me think he was familiar with the program. And I had always wanted what he had—to be a great writer. Even though he'd obviously drunk a lot early in his career, I know he didn't anymore. Something had changed his life. I could just tell there was something in his eyes that I recognized in my father's. And I wanted that.

By this time I also hadn't dated in a while, and I knew that was because of my drinking. It was like something was stamped on my face that said, "Stay away from this kid!" I knew it wasn't my looks or brains, and I had a good personality. Before, I had always figured it was my social status. I had come from nothing and had worked in restaurants all my life. That was easy money, but hard work. I thought if I had the right job, I'd get the right girl. But here I had a great job and *still* no relationship.

I told my idol about my desire be a writer and gave him a short story I'd written. He read it and liked it, but said I needed to work on my mechanics . . . although it was really good. He asked me what I was doing working as a production assistant if I wanted to be a writer. Well, I didn't know. I just wanted to work in the business. He told me that if I wanted to be a writer, what I needed to do was to go get some little job and write, period.

Unfortunately, it didn't take right away. I left Utah to work on another movie and kept on drinking. But I was hitting an emotional bottom. I'd get stoned or drunk and look at my computer and say, "What the hell am I doing? I want to write. But all I do is sit in front of the television or chase some friend so I can stash enough pot to avoid running out . . ."

My computer was sitting there. I didn't see me in front of it, and it stayed that way. I wasted *so* much time. It was just insanity.

So I finally decided to go back to AA, and it's been a great success. At age twenty-seven, I've been sober seven months and, like, five days. And in that time, I've written two original movie scripts and 350 pages of a novel, plus I rewrote another movie script that I wrote while drinking. So that's about six or seven hundred pages in seven months. I've read all these books on writing. There's something in me that wants to make up for all that wasted time. I want to so bad.

My computer is set up in a closet at a friend's house, and that's where I do all my writing. And I've been sleeping on a couch in that room for nine months now. The externals in my life haven't changed since I got sober, but I just don't care because I'm happy. I have a regular eight-to-five job with the city, which is easy. I have never had seven months of sobriety before. I've never written a book before, either.

I had a very real dream once where this person appeared and said, "You can have anything you want. But *only* if you stay sober." I know that is true for me.

The main difference in my life is that I don't drink. I still think way too much, but I don't run with it like I did. And I sleep, something I could never do. All my life I was unable to just lie down and go to sleep. My mind would run so fast with images, places, and people. Now I have an episode about once a week where I can't stop my thoughts. But the rest of the time I'm able to sleep pretty damn good.

I'm not tempted to pick up a six-pack or a joint. I have that romantic idea float by every once in a while of that cool time on a movie set with an old friend where I go, "Yeah, wasn't that fun!" But it's not that compulsion I used to have. That has pretty much left me. Even the last couple of times I drank, it was out of habit, instead of really wanting to. I know that's not what I truly want. What I want is to be in love, not only with myself, but with my writing, and to be in love with another person who has yet to come into my life.

I was looking for peace, but no matter how much I accomplished, I wasn't at peace because I still didn't like myself. That's why girls weren't attracted to me. I can see that now. And I'm beginning to develop some self-confidence. When I look at my writing, I still say that I'm not good enough; I don't have the talent to do this. But I don't care anymore; I'm going to do it anyway. I may not have the best vocabulary in the world or be a master of English, but what I have is the desire. I want to write stories.

If I send off my movie scripts or my book and hear nothing, I don't know what'll happen. What I do know is that I enjoy the shit out of it. I hope I wouldn't go back to drinking or smoking pot because that wouldn't be the answer to the problem. The answer would be to find a new path, to find something else that interests me. If I'm not meant to be a writer, and if I continue to work the program, it will be replaced with something else.

That is probably the only fear in my life right now. And I pray to God every single night, "Please make me a better writer, and if I'm not meant to be a writer, let me know what the hell I am supposed to do."

One big change is that my best friend from high school is sober. He's got two years and he's my sponsor. That's made an immense difference, to have somebody I trust be like a guiding light.


When my dad got sober, every single thing in his life changed. Before that, he had never owned a house, drove terrible cars, had no confidence, and was always a very pitiful person. Now he's retired from the phone company and has a home, two cars, and his own computer business. Dad is now incredibly humble. He no longer gets severely depressed or angry about anything. He's the happiest person in the world. As long as he doesn't get a six-pack in him, he always will be.

His first three years in sobriety I thought he was lying because he'd been such a drunk. "Right, Dad, you go to those meetings and then you're taking nips out in the car." I just didn't believe him. But AA became his way of life.

When I first stopped, nobody could believe it either, but for a different reason. Nobody I've ever worked with had any clue that I drank or smoked pot daily. Not even my mom. And the people who partied with me were, like, "Why, dude? I drink more than you do!"

I thought for the longest time in the world that I was not an alcoholic because I wasn't like my father. But the thing is, I don't think for me it had anything to do with what was going on in the outside of my life—I was able to juggle *that* with no problem. It was what was going on in the *inside.* And there's nothing on the outside that can fix that. It really is something spiritual that fixes us inside and then works itself out. And no matter what we have on the outside, it can only be made better if we fix the inside. But put everything you want on the outside, and if there's no inside, you'll still be hollow—it won't be worth a thing.

# 15

## I'VE GOT THE BOMB,
## WHEN DOES IT EXPLODE?

◪

Boys and girls raised in unstable surroundings are most likely to lose control of their drinking early. As we have seen, while instability in a child's home does not increase the *frequency* of addiction, the unstable environment does trigger an early and severe *onset*.[1] This can either have the tragic effect of leading quickly to flunked classes, lost jobs, arrests, illnesses, and eventual untimely death, or the beneficial outcome of early and lengthy sobriety.

Because of the severe symptoms suffered by teenagers and young adults from broken homes, many seek assistance early. Consequently, their long-term prognosis is better than even socially advantaged Harvard grads.[2]

Highly educated college students with relatively stable childhoods rarely manifest signs of trouble until later in life. They have the luxury of good food, excellent medical care, and strong social support to delay the full impact of this poison on their bodies. They typically show up at treatment centers in their early forties or in hospitals and cemeteries in their fifties.

### Isn't It About Time You Graduated?

In recent years, college students have significantly increased the amount of alcohol they drink at one time, resulting in escalating alcohol-related problems.[3] The emphasis for many students has shifted from social drinking to getting drunk. More than half of all men binge on five or more drinks. As for coeds, not long ago, only one in ten drank to get drunk; now, it's one out of every three.[4]

Drinking games, whose only purpose is inebriation, abound. So do parties and clubs conducive to bingeing on a smorgasbord of concoctions.

What does the future hold for these young men and women?

The bad news is that many of these students will end up addicted to alcohol. The good news is that the majority won't. Why? Because experience tells us that drinking problems in young people are often temporary, a normal and dangerous part of their subculture. In fact, those who suffer the most obvious social and behavioral problems from drinking—such as accidents, fights, and loss of friendships—are the *least* likely to have alcohol problems in middle age,[5] probably because they heed the early warning signs of excessive use.

Future problem drinkers come from a more subtle group whose attitudes and attachments to alcohol use aren't noticeable through negative behavior. They can cope well with increased consumption and suffer only minor consequences during their early drinking careers.[6]

While these drinkers continue to behave as always, most young adults, as we have seen, simply slow down and "graduate" from their heavy drinking behavior by their late twenties or early thirties.[7] And if you're like me and wonder what "slow down" means, consider that college students who don't become addicted exhibit *"major decreases in the quantity of alcohol consumed per occasion"* by age thirty. This natural change in behavior is a process that may include a new and stable marriage with increased responsibilities, an upwardly mobile job not surrounded by a drinking culture, or active church involvement.[8]

Those who don't change often receive social support for greater consumption from associates at work who party as a group,[9] from a circle of friends who regularly drink together, or from a heavy drinker with whom they are in a relationship at home. Many men and women continue to act as if they were still in college, long into their twenties and thirties. They continue to drink with the same or a similar group of friends, calling each other every week to plan the next weekend's drinking activity. Some consume a harmless amount of alcohol, while others use the group to "normalize" their excessive drinking behavior, as well as their regular hangovers. Many no longer remember the natural experience of awakening every morning feeling great, nor the satisfaction of operating at the true peak of their abilities.

For a while, changing social circles by switching jobs, friends, or lovers can still have a great influence on behavior.[10] But as a person gets older, the likelihood of a spontaneous decrease in drinking behavior naturally lessens.[11]

The most important point is that addiction to alcohol ordinarily involves a slow and lengthy development process.[12] The typical problem drinker, for example, is twenty-five to thirty-five years old, married, and working. His or her drinking is elastic and easily responds to various work or social conditions. By contrast, the typical alcoholic is thirty-five to forty-five years old, has an unstable marital history, and frequently stops drinking alcohol, but can't use it without problems for long.

The difference: One has been drinking alcohol regularly for ten more years.[13]

The message: Isn't it about time you graduated?

# 16

## TONY

Father was a driven man who got up at four every morning, read the *Wall Street Journal,* worked late, and then drank until he fell asleep. Mother indulged while cooking dinner. It wasn't obvious, but she always had a glass of Scotch going somewhere in the kitchen. It was never right in front of her, but you always knew she had a glass around, hidden away a bit.

Because Father was an angry man who disliked kids, we received many messages that there was something wrong with us. But no message was ever sent that there was anything wrong with alcohol.

In fact, about the third time I got drunk, the guys brought me home and stuffed me in Dad's Cadillac, which was parked in the garage. I woke up around four, realized where I was, and dragged myself to bed. At the breakfast table, Mother had aspirin and Alka-Seltzer for me, but not one word about "Don't get drunk." Just, "Here's what you do—take these."

I went to an all-boys private high school and discovered I was a good student, hardworking like my father—almost out of fear. Then on the weekends, I'd occasionally go out with the guys and get loaded.

I was an athlete, excelling at tennis, was president of the city-wide student organization, and active in many other groups. Some of my running buddies drank during the week, whereas I was pretty much a one-night-a-weekend kind of guy. But once I started drinking, I was like my friends and generally drank until the booze ran out.

In high school, I lived in fear of my father and acted mainly in response to that. Looking back, by the time I arrived at Stanford University, I possessed no tools for living. There I had to pick my own classes and figure out what to do and how to live. Eventually, I sank into depression, feeling I just couldn't make it.

My first year was awful. I slept a lot and started smoking the marijuana that was prevalent on campus. I hadn't smoked in high school but got into it in college. Needless to say, I quickly became a mediocre student. Then I got into writing—was just captivated by it—and that finally motivated me to make good grades, although not enough to quit drinking and smoking.

After graduation, I taught tennis, intending to take a year and write a novel. Instead, I moved in with my girlfriend, who also liked to drink and smoke dope, and that's essentially what I ended up doing that year.

After four months, I began to realize that my life was going downhill fast. So just to have a plan of some sort, I applied to law school, hoping to get direction in life, and was accepted for the following year. Once there, I discovered, to my chagrin, that I had to study much harder than before. In fact, there were periods of thirty, or even sixty, days when I did nothing but study, especially right before finals—work straight through, take the exams, then go out and get insanely drunk.

At the time, it seemed like everybody was doing that. They really weren't, but I had enough friends who were that it appeared that way. We'd party three days straight to blow off finals.

Then I went to NYU and got a master's in tax law. I had broken up with my girlfriend and wanted to get out of town, so I decided on New York. There the pattern was the same—study like crazy, get smashed after finals.

Alcohol became the only thing I was using because marijuana wasn't really working that well, and I didn't want to get arrested. But in my mind, alcohol was OK. It was the acceptable drug.

Then I fell in love with a woman in New York, and we moved to New Mexico, where I started a law practice. Soon after that, Beth was accepted into graduate school in North Carolina and moved. So I was living alone, practicing law, working basically from eight to eight. When I came home, I'd get a six-pack of beer, turn on the TV, drink my six-pack, and go to bed—developing a pattern of drinking at night, alone.

When Beth came back from North Carolina, we moved to the San Francisco Bay Area, and married. By this time, my pattern of nightly drinking was set.


In the Bay Area, I began imagining myself to be a wine connoisseur. I ran into all these guys who were experts in Napa Valley wines, and I got into Bordeaux and other French wines as well. So I started a wine cellar and hung out with people who were gourmets and fancied themselves wine connoisseurs, too.

We had these weekend dinners where everyone talked about the wine and the food—on and on into the night. Somehow it was socially acceptable to have champagne before dinner, white wine with the first course, red during the second, and port with dessert. Then I advanced to smoking cigars and drinking cognac. It was all so socially proper, though the total quantities were huge.

During the week, it was still mostly just me, either watching television or reading, and drinking wine—my wife and the babies upstairs asleep. Sometimes I'd drag myself to bed by ten or eleven; other times I'd sit there and drink until midnight. Occasionally, I'd wake up in the morning still on the couch.

Every night I began by planning to have just two glasses of wine with dinner. Eventually, I had to admit to myself that I was going to have a bottle of wine during the meal. For years I thought I *was* having a bottle, but in keeping track of my wine cellar I noticed the inventory decreasing rapidly. So the numbers didn't add up. I clearly was having more than a bottle a night.

Then I went through a time with my cellar when I'd say, "OK, I'm *not* going to buy any more wine. I'll drink everything that's down there." (And I probably had two to three thousand bottles.) "I'm gonna drink that, and when that's done, I quit. That's it, I'm done!"

So then I would go for six months without buying any. Then I would look at my forlorn wine cellar with its increasingly empty racks and go, "Oh, God!" So I'd research the best bargains and begin accumulating wine again.

After a while, I'd exclaim, *"No,* I can't be buying all this wine." I'd glance into the cellar and think, "If I drink all that, it'll probably kill me. But I can't *not* drink all that wine 'cause I bought it. And I bought it to drink, *not* to save, or collect, or to make money."

Obviously, I had become somewhat obsessed with the cellar, as well as the epicurean lifestyle that accompanied it. But my health was getting terrible—I'd basically gained a hundred pounds in eight years. At home I had become the chef so that Beth could play with the kids while I cooked and drank my wine. And I was eating these huge gourmet meals.

Although I had been an agile athlete in many sports, I got in such bad shape that I couldn't even run. Finally, my brother, who was one year older, had a heart attack at age thirty-eight. He was president of his local food and wine society and, like me, weighed 265 pounds. His myocardial infarction scared the crap out of me.

I'd been waking up hungover every morning feeling terrible, but I knew not to drink in the morning because alcoholics did that. And I never drank at lunch because I'd either have to take a nap or keep on drinking. So I had my regimen locked down: *I don't drink until 5:30 or 6:00.*

But in the mornings, I had to do something about the way I felt, so I took Mylanta, Pepto-Bismol, Alka-Seltzer, or whatever. And I'd have the strongest coffee on earth—I even ordered a 220-volt espresso machine from Italy, although it required me to rewire the kitchen, because I needed the real stuff.

I'd gotten in a hot tub once and thought it cured my hangover. So I also had one of those installed and soaked in it for half an hour on especially bad mornings. Truth is, none of that really worked. It was all just something to try. The only thing that works is not taking the first drink. But I certainly wasn't ready for that.

After my brother's heart attack, I decided to check out cardiovascular disease because I felt so bad that I was fearful of having my own heart attack. Stanford University had an excellent heart disease prevention program, but I didn't actually enroll because I wanted no one to know I might have a problem. I wanted to be perfect, you know. I was never able to say I had faults of any kind—

I came from a family where you didn't ask for help and you never admitted weakness. So I quietly bought Stanford's tapes, and with their help was slowly able to change my diet and begin exercising.

Part of the program specified a maximum of two drinks a night *on average,* and *never* more than five drinks in any one night. So I began tracking my drinking with a chart. Every morning, I'd reconstruct the night before: "Well, let's see. I had that bottle. And I had a couple of beers before that . . . and I think I had that other bottle . . . I think." In any event, I was sure that was over five. So I'd put a six on the chart. Then the following day I'd find myself writing another six, which only left two drinks for the week to make the fourteen average. So I'd say, "Screw it. I'm not gonna keep track this week. I'll do it *next* week."

And then I tried other systems. "OK, I won't drink Monday through Thursday," I'd decide. "I'll just drink on Friday and Saturday." I'd make it on Monday with all the willpower I had. Then Tuesday, I'd think, *Well, I did so well yesterday, and I want to try out that new cabernet—I'll just have two glasses of that with dinner.* But after a couple, the thought would occur, *Well, I could just finish the bottle.* Once I did that, then I was back to sitting on the couch, in front of the TV, staring out the window, drinking.

By Wednesday night, I would say, "Well, screw it, I already drank on Tuesday; I might as well drink tonight." Two weeks later, I'd think, *Wait a minute! You were gonna cut down on your drinking.* So then I'd try out some new routine.

One of them involved having one drink every 40 minutes. I knew I wanted to sit at home in the evening and have something to drink over a couple of hours. So I divided 120 minutes by the three drinks I wanted and resolved to have only one drink every 40 minutes. But that didn't work because after the first 40-minute drink, the next one would be gone in 20, followed by the usual "Screw it."

After coming up with a number of these systems, I found that none worked—and got really scared about my drinking.

What scared me the most was that I had met something that I couldn't conquer on my own. In the past, for example, when I went through law school, even though I basically hated it, I could get through on willpower. I even made good grades—honor roll and all that crap. Before, I had always been able to put my mind and effort into anything and at least make progress, eventually arriving where I wanted. But I was starting to see that I wasn't going to be able to make a dent in my drinking. If today were Sunday, I couldn't tell you whether I'd be drinking on Tuesday or not. That was frightening to me because in my mind I had always believed that I could quit at any time and that I *chose* to drink every night.

"I just *like* drinking," I'd say. "It's fun, a good thing to do, and I'm *choosing* to drink every night." It never occurred to me that someone who was exercising choice might choose to go to the movies some night completely sober, or might choose to read a book without having a drink, or all the other things you can do. Why would they choose night after night to drink? That had never crossed my mind.

When I wrote a schedule in advance and put it on paper, I started seeing that I wasn't really making this choice. I would choose the amount I would drink, or choose to drink on some nights but not on others—and then the results were the exact opposite of what I chose. So it was scary.


By this time, I had quit practicing law and was totally making my living playing the stock market. I did have some real estate, a little bit of oil-and-gas interests, and some bonds, but my money was almost all in stocks, mostly U.S., but some international.

I had become an investor when Beth inherited some money. I was working as a tax adviser to some entrepreneurs, and had learned a little about investing from those guys. When I started playing with Beth's inheritance, the market turned up and I got lucky.

At the time I didn't realize it was luck, but I had a hell of a run for about five years, and we made a ton of money. Then came the big downturn in the stock market, and I plunged far and fast and got panicky. During that time, I became aware of reacting to the fear by consciously saying to myself, "I've gotta drink." And I would drink until I no longer felt the fear or anything else.

I was already afraid of living in California, with the earthquakes, mud slides, and crime. But the market's falling apart, and my response to it, alarmed me.

It was a weird time, with round-the-clock stress, because I was following the Japanese market, too, and that opens in the middle of the night here. So I would drink, sleep a few nervous hours, jump up to see what was happening to the Japanese market, and then try to go back to sleep again—terrified that we were going broke.

I felt trapped. The stock market was in the toilet and headed lower, but I felt paralyzed—afraid to take my losses and fearful of holding on. Then there was the wine cellar. I kept looking at it and thinking, *What am I going to do with that thing? I've got to drink it. I bought it—but if I drink it, it'll kill me.*

Selling the wine cellar or giving it away never occurred to me. Not once. In sobriety, I eventually gave it to a shelter for homeless alcoholics, and they sold it for a sum that enabled them to completely remodel their building and add more beds. In the end, the cellar turned out to be a gift of some sort.

But then I was still trapped, and I started to see that—which was an improvement. I had been in the trap for a long time, but I had never been aware of it. When I finally attempted to pass its limits, I was surprised to find that there were these invisible walls I couldn't get through.

That same year my second son was born. When Beth had our oldest son, we had gone to the hospital at noon, and I was sober when he was delivered that night. With my second son, she didn't start having contractions until late at night, so I was already intoxicated when we went to the hospital. I was mortified that I was drunk while this event was happening. This child I dearly wanted to bring into the world was being born, and here I was, in the midst of all these nurses and doctors, knowing that I just reeked of alcohol. I couldn't believe I did that.

The next week, when I made my usual list—"clean the yard, buy potato chips, get a new hose"—I added, "buy books on alcoholism." That was on there for months, representing my intention to look into it.

Finally, after watching myself drink for a year-and-a-half, and realizing that I couldn't control it, I got the opportunity to look into a mirror. We visited my family over the Christmas holidays, and being conscious of my own drinking, I noticed theirs, too, and realized that a couple of them were clearly addicted to alcohol. I could just see it—and I knew it ran in families.

The very next day, I went to the bookstore, but I was as self-conscious of buying a book on alcoholism as a teenager buying his first condom. I thought, *If they ask me, I'll tell them it's not for me.* Can you imagine? "The rubbers are for a friend." Yeah, you bet.

Standing at the counter, I wished the book's title weren't so obvious. The truth was that nobody really cared. They could have been selling cans of green beans. Yet I could feel the sweat beginning to drip under my arms.

The book recommended going to a treatment center and, after that, to AA. But I wasn't going to treatment because I probably wasn't an alcoholic. I could be, but everybody would think I was for sure if I went to a treatment center. I also wouldn't go to AA because I was certain it was pretty much street people and others who had no lives—certainly not the kind of people *I* would ever relate to.

Not liking that advice, I went and bought another book. This one said, "Go to therapy and to AA." But people in my family don't go to therapy because we don't have anything wrong with us.

Then I bought a third book, written by an AA guy who said, "Go to AA."

Of all the books I read, none said, "Do it on your own." None said, "Stay home and use this self-help book." None even remotely suggested you could solve this problem yourself. Every one of them had this message: *Go somewhere and do something and talk to people.*

So I dragged myself to an AA meeting—in Piedmont, of course, the wealthiest section of Oakland. No way was I going to a meeting in downtown Oakland with the vagrants. I got all dressed up and discovered after I got there that most of the people didn't even *live* in Piedmont! They just attended that meeting because they liked it.

I didn't understand a word that was said. But at the end of the meeting, a guy came up to me and mentioned that he'd just gotten back from Thailand and told me about all the fun he'd had. He asked how was I doing and seemed like the kind of guy I drank with. And he had been to Thailand, so apparently he wasn't like a street person. And he thought life was fun. I could relate to him as a guy I could hang out with.

He got a copy of the meeting schedule for the whole city, circled a bunch of good meetings, and handed it to me. So I went once or twice a week for about four months, which was enough to not drink. But I was flipping out—my anxiety level was unbelievable.

I had not realized what a big role alcohol played in my life. At night I used it as my whole system of relating to my wife, the kids, and my friends. I was feeling alcohol, and I wasn't feeling anything else. Then in the morning and most of the day I was hung over. So it had been a long, long time since I'd actually experienced my own feelings. When I began to feel, the sensation was frightening. As children, our feelings were regulated; in my family we had to act a certain way and not express how we felt. So this was the first time in my life that my feelings weren't censored or medicated.

And I had no tools to cope.

What I hadn't realized about the drinking was that it had to some extent controlled my fears about life. Plus, I had suppressed guilt about some things I'd done, like showing up drunk at the hospital when my son was born, and all sorts of other things.

What finally helped was that I began attending a meeting that was specifically aimed at studying the twelve steps of AA.* There I heard a guy say that he was at the place where he was thinking about either drinking again or killing himself, or he was going to do the fourth step. I had been contemplating killing myself or drinking again, and that was the first time I had heard of an alternative. So I got that in my mind—you can do these steps—and I got a sponsor and told him how anxious I was.

"Well, that's normal," he said. "When you first get sober, your anxiety level is high. That's how we all felt. You're only just about to change your *entire life,* you know. And you're a 'tweener. Your old way of living doesn't work anymore, and you haven't learned the new way yet. So you *ought* to be anxious." It was true.

So we worked the steps together. And that fifth step, when I told him all my secrets—what a catharsis! There were things I told

---

*The twelve steps are set out in the appendix.

this guy I had never told anybody—*ever*—and wasn't gonna. I mean, I was going to *die* with this stuff. What a relief just to tell somebody!

Then, getting to the eighth and ninth step, I was able to make amends to some people I'd never intended to talk to the rest of my life. I was able to track them down and tell them how I had been wrong or confess to them whatever I had done, and let the chips fall.

None of the people are my close friends now, but the guilt is gone. And the ones I had nightmares about, those dreams are gone. It's like cleaning my side of the street. When I did that, most of my anxiety magically disappeared.


I had several good years of sobriety when my marriage failed. It hadn't worked for years before I got sober and didn't get any better after. I had stayed, but it was actually part of the old way of living.

I thought if I worked the steps thoroughly, I would be able to be with her. And I used to read that story in the Big Book, "Doctor, Alcoholic, Addict," where the doctor talks about his relationship with his wife and how he came to see her good qualities. When he focused on them, they magnified. When he focused on her negatives, they grew.

*There's something in here that can change the way I see this woman,* I would think. *Somehow, we're going to make it.* I was looking for the result of that story, which is that the doctor and his wife have been together now some twenty-seven years since he got sober. But what it really says is that you have to accept life on life's terms—accept it just the way it is. And "just the way it was" for us was that we were not compatible; we had been that way for a long time, and it wasn't going to get better.

So that's what the last year has been about—getting divorced and working through that. Before making the decision, I did another fourth step around my relationship with my wife, and it was helpful. No matter how hard I tried, I wasn't able to see what *I* was doing in the marriage, *my* part in it, and I realized that was because I didn't want to continue. I just didn't want to be doing it anymore.

I remember leaving my sponsor's house, thinking on the way home, *The only way for you to stop behaving this way is to get divorced. Your behavior is prompted by the fact that you're locked into this place you don't want to be in.* But by the time I got home, my mind had shifted to: *We've got to do couple's counseling. That's what will help. We* can *fix this. We* can solve *this.*

We went, but it didn't help.


Despite some events, like the divorce, my four years of sobriety have been a wonderful experience. I have never had the kind of friends I have now—people I can talk to about what's actually happening with me.

I enjoy being of service, especially by working with people who are just coming in and feel lost. When I'm able to give them something small to do, like a short daily reading, and get them talking about their lives, they can get better.

Ironically, AA has become the main focus of my life in many ways because it's where my heart is. The guy who wanted nothing to do with AA for fear of the lowlifes now has a whole range of people as best friends. I relate to people now whom I would never have spent time with before, because we *are* related on a very human level.

I had prejudices I didn't know I had against people who weren't in a certain social class. I've learned a lot from these men and women, whose lives are so much better than mine, because they have principles, and they live according to certain truths. That's what I want. I've done the money thing—had large amounts of it—and ended up wanting to kill myself.

I lived for years in a city that is half-black, half-white, but all my friends were white. It wasn't until I got to AA that I started having black friends. Now I attend meetings where most people are black, and we feel comfortable with each other and have become good friends, even though our lives are totally different.

It's refreshing to be a part of the human race, the *whole* human race.


What I would tell someone who is successful financially and drinks more often than they really want, is that *there's a choice.* It doesn't seem like it, but there is. For one thing, it's possible to quit drinking and have a lot of fun.

But I won't say it's easy, because there's a barrier you've got to go through. You have to recognize that alcohol just isn't doing for you what it once did. For years, it is the fuel for the party, but eventually it just turns into a depressant.

You have to grab onto the hope that there's a good life without alcohol. I don't know if anybody will get this, but there are opportunities to expand yourself as a human being that you can't even imagine. You can't fathom how much bigger life is when you're feeling, when you let others enter your life in a real way and be a part of it, and when you allow yourself to hear people tell the truth about what's really going on in their lives.

Initially, I was amazed at meetings. I couldn't believe people would actually talk about what they were talking about. *Why don't these people just shut up?* I remember thinking. *Don't they know that other people are hearing what they're saying?* And then I realized that I was hearing *truth* for the first time.

Now I know more about what really happens in the lives of people I've known for three months than I know about the lives of guys I grew up with. It's astonishing.

It ends our lonely existence, that's for sure. Toward the end of my drinking, I was terribly lonely and couldn't admit that to anybody. I had a few friends and we'd go out, but we never talked about real things—we just drank together and went home. If we went to a party, I'd get into conversations and try not to talk about much of anything, not let anyone know what I was thinking. There was no contact. Then, when sitting in front of the TV, drinking beer or wine, I would occasionally get a glimmer of what I was feeling— and I was lonely, real lonely.

Today it can get nuts with the phone ringing and all kinds of things going on, including my buddies calling to go camping or backpacking or skiing.

Many of my friends are recovering drinkers and none of us were great at relationships, so we're having to work our friendships out. For example, when I was depressed from going through the divorce, a friend needed a hand, but he became a little pushy and I had to tell him to back off. "I just can't be there for you this week," I told him. "I'm down, and I want to be left alone."

In the past, I would have made up some reason for being unable to help, and then I would have dropped the friendship because I couldn't deal with confrontation on such a personal level. It was difficult for me to say, "What you're doing is bugging me." I took things so personally that I figured all my friends did, too.

It was also hard for me to talk about my role in a situation where I had perhaps done something that justifiably pissed somebody off.

The ability to take an upsetting event or situation and put it on the table, outside of ourselves, for both of us to look at, is a wonderful gift. I can look at my role and they can look at theirs, and we can discuss it and own our part in it without having it become personal to either of us. It's wonderful to be with people who are willing to look at their side, who are able to admit they have faults, and who can see that they perhaps contributed to the situation.

My old tendency was to minimize, or simply deny, the fact that I had done something, or to react with, "Why are you being so damn sensitive?" To put the other person down, instead of saying, "OK, that did happen. I did that, and I'm willing to look at it." In the end, by practicing honesty, you become better friends.

The man with no tools for living is learning how to live.

# 17

## WAKE-UP CALL FOR WOMEN

■

Drinking is especially dangerous for women. They suffer heart, liver, and brain damage after drinking less—and for a shorter time—than men. A woman's risk of liver cirrhosis becomes significant when she averages just two drinks a day. An increase in breast cancer is also associated with that level of consumption.[1] With recent increases in young women's consumption, a disaster is slowly unfolding in a generation of unsuspecting women.

Women's bodies process alcohol differently than men's, and the distinction is not good news. When a man and woman are given the same amount to drink, we'd expect the woman to be more intoxicated due to size differences. And we'd be right. But we'd never anticipate that her blood alcohol would be significantly higher even after adjusting for weight.[2] As a result, *a typical woman having two to four drinks is at least 50 percent more intoxicated than her larger male companion.*

"Why does that matter?" you might ask. "She's just having more fun for the same price."

Unfortunately, we tend to forget that alcohol is a toxic substance capable of injuring vital organs. Our bodies don't welcome alcohol; indeed, they fight to prevent its entry into the river of life—the bloodstream. The first defense is mounted in the stomach, followed by a battle in the liver. Any woman, however, is at a distinct disadvantage compared to a man because her body is not as capable of protecting itself. Her stomach is only 23 percent as effective as a man's in neutralizing alcohol. As a result, more toxin directly enters the bloodstream.[3]

With repeated excessive use, alcohol destroys the stomach's

ability to combat its passage. Where men lose *half* of their capacity, women lose theirs almost *completely.* That loss of protection by the stomach is temporarily felt by any woman who fasts when she drinks in order to avoid combining alcohol and food calories. The situation is so bad that there's practically no difference in her blood level whether she drinks alcohol or has it injected directly into her bloodstream. The body simply has no defense.[4]

How serious is this problem? The first extended study of female alcoholics ever conducted was done in St. Louis, Missouri. Researchers there located 100 women eleven years after their discharge from the hospital for treatment of alcoholism—and found 31 percent dead. They died at a rate 4.5 times greater than normal. The life expectancy of the general female population in St. Louis was 66.5 years; the average age at death of these female alcoholics was 51—*their life span had been shortened by fifteen years.* Most frightening, the death rate for women under age 34 was almost fourteen times greater than normal.[5]

Studies in France, Australia, Britain, and the U.S. confirm a significantly higher rate of severe liver disease in women after drinking less and for a shorter time than men.[6]

CT scans reveal that women's brains are also more sensitive to alcohol. A woman's ventricles—the empty spaces in the brain—become enlarged from abuse more quickly and with less consumption.[7] Given this accelerated affect on the brain, it is not surprising that women with half the drinking history of men perform as poorly on tests of recall, perceptual accuracy, and problem solving.[8] Luckily, such brain abnormalities begin recovering with abstinence, and it appears that women's brains recover faster and more completely than men's.[9]

A study of women in Barcelona, Spain, published in 1995 in *The Journal of the American Medical Association* found that women's hearts are also significantly more sensitive to the damaging effects of alcohol. The women drank heavily daily, which is not unusual in Spain. Most worked, all had stable employment histories, few ever acted drunk, and none engaged in binge drinking. Yet their hearts pumped significantly less blood than normal, and they suffered the same heart damage as men with far less consumption.[10]

Besides liver, brain, and heart damage, women also suffer from anemia, obesity, and gastrointestinal problems after a significantly shorter period of heavy drinking.[11]

Women are vulnerable, not only because their bodies provide significantly less protection, but also because of the secrecy that often surrounds a woman's addiction to alcohol.

The secrecy has a lengthy tradition, likely originating in the world's historical antipathy toward female drinking. In Roman times, for example, female drinking was not only illegal but punishable by death.[12] Most cultures, though, simply used social taboos, rather than laws, to curb the practice. Even today, many older women reflect their own generation's standards by silently disapproving of drinking by young ladies.

This overly protective past did contain wonderful benefits. The genetic bomb carried by many women failed to explode due to forced abstinence and limited exposure to alcohol. And women without a family history of alcoholism were often unable to engage in the years of heavy social drinking that can lead to alcohol dependence. As a result, women's observed rates of addiction have always been significantly lower than men's.

But the dangerous impact of this heritage is that women became more secretive in their drinking, and suffered greater anxiety and depression, as well as lower self-esteem, than men.[13] With the stigma attached to excessive female drinking, women also sought help more reluctantly.[14] Oblivious to their greater physical vulnerability to alcohol, many waited until it was too late. And researchers, convinced that alcohol addiction was essentially a male disorder, studied men and their sons almost exclusively.

In recent years, many women who otherwise would likely have been closet problem drinkers took the more acceptable route of using tranquilizers and sedatives—taking Valium during the day instead of a drink, or a sleeping pill at bedtime in lieu of a nightcap.[15] The practice became so prevalent that 11 percent of U.S. adults once carried a prescribed tranquilizer.[16] The Rolling Stones even wrote a song about it called "Mother's Little Helper."

Why would women choose tranquilizers? Because barbiturates and benzodiazepines, such as Valium, are part of the alcohol family. Their pharmacology is similar. As proof of their commonality, witness the fact that every withdrawal syndrome can be relieved by the consumption of the withdrawn drug—and that alcohol-withdrawal symptoms can be ended by taking a tranquilizer, and vice versa.[17]

Young women today are out of their doctors' offices and into the clubs and pubs, which have discovered that welcoming them in large numbers attracts men and profits. And if it is true that some women, like men, carry genetic bombs that explode with significant exposure to alcohol, and that others become addicted through years of excessive use, we would expect a substantial increase in women's rates of addiction as cultural changes lift relevant taboos. That is exactly what we see.

## Conclusion

In recent years, countless women have cast aside archaic stigmas against female drinking. In doing so, it is doubtful that they appreciate the greater vulnerability of their hearts, brains, and livers to the ravages of alcohol.

# 18

## JESSICA

I fell in love with drinking at thirteen. Friday nights, a whole bunch of us kids would get together, and I'd have two beers and be loaded. My family thought I was just doing kid stuff because I was an absolute sweetheart—excellent grades, president of the class, cheerleader . . . Little Susie High School. But I got plowed just about every weekend, because it was a blast.

I went to Fairfield College, a small Jesuit school where the demographics were cookie cutter. Everybody was upper-middle-class Irish or Italian. I have fond memories of Fairfield. I continued to excel as a student there. Also, I had my first serious boyfriend, taught ballet, and partied on weekends.

But after two years, I decided to transfer to Boston University to major in chemical engineering.

BU had over 20,000 students, and the first time I set foot in the dorm, they handed me a pamphlet entitled "How to avoid rape on campus." And I'm going, "Huh?" I was clueless. Twenty-one years old and thought I knew everything, but with no idea how incredibly naive I was.

All my classes at BU were in engineering 'cause I had to cram them into the last two years. That would have been tough enough if you were trying to stay sober, but I wasn't trying. I was out partying in the middle of the week. It was the best escape I could find.

I missed Fairfield, and I couldn't stay up with all the assigned homework, which scared me to death. But rather than stay home and work, it was easier to forget about it by going out, and that made it cyclical. How the hell I even passed is beyond me. I went from a 4.0 student to barely getting my degree.

I didn't intend for it to be that way. I thought it was just typical college partying—fun stuff—and I absolutely loved to party. It was always social, never by myself, because at school you can always find somebody to go to the pub with you. We drank mostly beer or wine—the cheap stuff, whatever we could afford, with lots of pitchers.

I didn't date much at BU. Basically, it was me and my girl-friends, and we watched out for each other 'cause college scenes with a bunch of drunk students can get ugly. I had guys as good buddies who told me things I should never have heard—about just how rotten men could be when it came to women—and I was scared to death of being somebody's story to a whole group of guys, so I just stayed away from 'em.

After college, I went to work for a semiconductor manufacturer as a process engineer. At first, I bought a bottle of Tanqueray because Tanqueray and tonic had become my drink. But when I realized how fast I was going through it, I thought, *I can't be doing this. This is my first job out of college, and if I start drinking during the week, I'm gonna screw it up. I'll just drink on the weekend.* And that's what I did for a long time. But even then I noticed that my tolerance for alcohol had increased substantially. In going out to dinner with friends, I always seemed to drink more than them—but I was *able* to drink more, so it was no problem.

I taught aerobics four nights a week and remember thinking of it as a way to keep me from drinking. So I knew way back then that I had a tendency to drink too much, but I didn't regard it as serious. I just drank more than most people.

Most Fridays, our whole group of young engineers would hit a Happy Hour that had a buffet and a band. I usually didn't eat much, though. Knowing I was consuming so many calories drinking, I couldn't do a whole lot of eating, too. We'd usually close the place at one or two in the morning, and I never kept track of how many I had, but the idea of having just four or five drinks over eight hours was never my thing, particularly when I assumed that the bars made their drinks so weak.

I kept in mind that's what everybody did, and many people did seem to drink like me—and I, of course, gravitated toward them. So I kept on telling myself that it was OK and that it was normal.

After two years, I changed employers, and that's when my drinking progressed. I moved to a small town in Massachusetts, where my company was the only employer. Everybody born there went to work at my company, married their high school sweetheart, and lived happily ever after. And here I was, a single, twenty-five-year-old woman—and instead of the young engineers I was used to, all the new guys were in their fifties.

Though I was there for only a year, I just hated it. These older guys had been in engineering for years and never took me seriously. Plus there was my wonderful social life. But out in the middle of nowhere, I lucked into this couple—Jim and Darlene. He was fifty-six, she was twenty-three, and both loved to drink.

When I called on an ad, looking for an apartment, Jim said, "Well, we're just sitting around here having a beer. Come join us and check it out." So I went and had a beer with them, and we hit it off immediately. After I began renting their downstairs apartment, they became my social circle, and that's when I started drinking during the week. I'd come home from work, go upstairs, and drink wine with them.

That routine began affecting my punctuality at work. I was supposed to be there at 7:15 A.M., and that's tough for me even now that I'm sober.

I also started drinking by myself sometimes, when I was in my apartment, alone. I'd tell myself, "Well, you know, Jim and Darlene are having a beer, too. It's not my fault that I don't know anybody to invite over in this one-horse town."

And I began playing games with it, saying, "OK, I won't drink for the next few days," and I wouldn't and feel great. Then it would be Friday and time to start up again. Then I'd get into drinking until it was causing trouble again, and it was time to stop a little.

The trouble at that point was limited to getting to work late. It wasn't causing any major problems that I saw, but it was starting to make me nervous. I realized that I was thinking too much about how to control it. And I knew that drinking a half a bottle of gin was not what normal people did when they had a couple of drinks at home after work.

Then I got involved with a financial consultant living in California—a guy I met while he was at an investment training program in Boston. He was such a gentleman—attentive and nice. So when my company sent me to California on a business trip, I called him and we got together.

That started this whirlwind, coast-to-coast romance, a real sweep-you-off-your-feet sort of thing. He'd call me and say, "Honey, I just have to see you! There's a ticket waiting for you at the airport." So I'd be flying out there just for the weekend, or he'd be coming to see me.

*Well, he has to be in love with me,* I thought, *because he wouldn't be putting all this effort into somebody 3,000 miles away.* But what I didn't realize at the time—nor find out until after I was married to the slimeball—was that he was married, and his wife was pregnant with his second baby. He had a little bachelor pad on the side and pretended that was his home when I'd go out to visit. We were always going on these excursions out of town, which I thought were so romantic, but he, of course, couldn't chance running into people.

I fell deeply in love and decided to quit my miserable job and move to Los Angeles to be with him. I must have been in a Cinderella mode because part of me thought that being with him would help my drinking. He wasn't a big drinker, and I thought, *Well, of course, I'm not gonna drink like I have been because he wouldn't go for that. I won't want to disappoint him.* Also, I wouldn't be living by myself anymore, so I couldn't drink the way I had been. It wasn't just me and a bottle of Tanqueray across the room—there was somebody else in the picture who wouldn't be too psyched about my pouring a drink regularly.

We got engaged, and I was on top of the world. But every once in a while there was a flash of something unsettling. One time his oldest daughter said to me, "Mommy and Daddy are getting divorced."

*They're already divorced,* I would think, and say, "Steve, what's the scoop here? Emily's talking about Mom and Dad getting a divorce, and . . ."

"Jessie, she's a four-year-old. She doesn't understand."

"OK."

After we were married, I started questioning when he actually got divorced, 'cause he had to explain this youngest baby—and he had told me that the reason he and his wife had split up was because she'd had an affair and had gotten pregnant by another man.

Everything he said to me seemed plausible at the time, and I bought it because I wanted to. The alternative—because his lies were so ugly—was unfathomable. Did that mean that he was really married while we were engaged? Did that mean that this little girl was his baby? If the answers were "Yes," that meant I was in love with a man who had no conscience whatsoever, and I couldn't believe that. So I would tell myself, "Well, I've got to give him the benefit of the doubt. He's my husband, you know. I have to believe him."

We had a lot of fun as newlyweds. We'd run to Laguna Beach for the afternoon, have margaritas and Mexican food, then come home and sit in the Jacuzzi with gin-and-tonics. On normal nights, we'd have drinks before and during dinner but never afterwards, so I would find a way to make dinner last for three hours. He would have two light drinks, but anytime I made them, mine would be Tanqueray, Tanqueray, Tanqueray, and tonic. A couple of times, he accidentally took a sip of mine and said, "Whoa!"

Whenever we went out, I always wanted to keep on drinking. At a restaurant, I'd talk him into ordering a second bottle of wine, which was not something he would have done. I got him to drink more than he ever had, and he would joke, "God, I'm going to end up an alcoholic, hanging around with you."

My drinking became less controlled as the red flags were beginning to go up, signaling, "You can't trust this man." I began worrying that there might be other women. I was a sales rep in the semiconductor industry, which required me to travel, and I'd call home and wouldn't be able to get hold of him. When I'd confront him, he'd say, "Let's have a drink and talk about it." Looking back on it now, that was an easy way to manipulate me and I wouldn't be thinking as clearly.

One time, I stayed up and called home all night with no answer. There were phones all over the house, including one on the nightstand by the bed, so I wondered what his excuse would be. When I finally reached him at work, he told me, "I was so exhausted that I just slept and slept and didn't hear the phone."

Another time he claimed to have stayed at his brother's. Then we saw his brother the following week and he acted like he hadn't seen my husband in ages.

But he was very good at turning things around, making me feel guilty for not trusting him and always thinking the worst. He'd make me feel like a paranoid and insecure woman.

So finally I got fed up enough to where I said, "Maybe I'm paranoid, maybe I'm crazy, but I'm going to a counselor and find out." It was just getting too painful, and I was drinking a whole lot more because I was so scared to look at the possibility that I had chosen as a lifetime partner a man who, if this stuff I was thinking was true, was pretty reprehensible. I was also afraid of what a divorce would do to me monetarily because I had given him all of my money to handle since he was a financial consultant. Another brilliant move! He couldn't even handle his *own* money.

When I started talking about going for counseling, he got scared because he figured that any objective person would tell me, "You're not nuts, lady. He's screwing around."

The shit finally hit the fan when I came home from a Thanksgiving visit with my parents. He had refused to come, forfeiting a nonrefundable ticket, because he knew that my family would give me direct advice and support. By the time I returned to California, he had apparently decided that his secret life would end the marriage, and he might as well make the first move. So he had the locks changed on our house—he had locked me out of my own home!

I went to a budget hotel, bought a bottle of cheap wine, and sat watching television, thinking that my marriage was over.


For a few days I became the house guest of two very dear friends, Brenda and her husband, which was so embarrassing because I *had* to drink. He didn't drink and Brenda had an occasional glass of wine, so after work I found reasons to go to a movie, or shopping, or out to dinner—so I could drink. I felt bad about it because these people were being gracious, and I was so ashamed that I couldn't stop.

My husband almost convinced me to come back by seeing a counselor himself. Here was a guy who would lie about whether there was orange juice in the fridge, but he sounded so sincere that I thought we might be able to keep our marriage together.

He arranged for us to have dinner and talk, and he bought champagne and Tanqueray, probably thinking, *If I can get her to start drinking, then take her home to bed, we're back!* Although that old trick didn't work, he did get me to thinking that he could change.

Then he used the girls, who were now four and eight, as another way to get me to the house. "The kids are here," he said, "and they need to see you." The girls didn't know what was going on, so I stopped by for them. Then he asked me to drop them off at their mother's because he didn't think I had the guts to talk to her—his big mistake.

On seeing her, I said, "I really need to know when you and Steve actually split up."

Her eyebrows went up. "Well, it was after you two started seeing each other," she replied. I felt like a mule had kicked me in the stomach.

"Oh, no." I began shaking involuntarily. "He t-told me he was di-divorced," I stuttered. "I had no . . . I had no . . . idea he was *married.*"

She was incredibly gracious. "I figured something like that happened," she said. "At first I thought you were the kind of woman who didn't mind breaking up a family. But when I saw you with my kids, I knew it had to be him . . . lying to you, the way he lied to me." We both started crying, and she told me, "He started going to Boston on business when I was five months pregnant, and he would spend many weekends here out of town. But what could I do with a four-year-old and my baby on the way? He got mad at me for even thinking he'd do something like that."

The most reprehensible thing is that this guy denied being this beautiful little girl's father. I went back to the house, popped a bottle of champagne, and left him a glass with a note that said, "Here's one to the divorce, baby."

And I never went back.

That was the beginning of the end for me, because I began living by myself again. The divorce was ugly, and I was now drinking like a fish, while living in a world of hurt. I had just been promoted to a top management job that required me to be in the office every day. I was used to sales jobs where I could set my own hours, drink like I wanted, see a few customers, and make it look like I was working. As long as sales went up, nobody noticed. But now, while being ripped apart emotionally, I needed to act responsibly—but I just couldn't. Sometimes I'd show up at nine or ten, then leave for a long lunch at noon. Luckily my boss officed in New Jersey, so that could continue for a while. But then he started making demands on me, like expecting me to be at work on time.

Besides the emotional strain of the divorce, the financial pressure became unbearable. I leased an apartment, rented furniture, and still paid the mortgage on the house my ex was in. He refused to pay, so it would be lost through foreclosure if I didn't. I couldn't afford both, so my folks loaned me money, which I'm still paying back.

As you can imagine, I've only had a couple of dates since. For a while I had such a chip on my shoulder that my sister called me "the date from hell." But I had no feelings then. I was just numb—and wanted to stay that way.

There were only six of us in the office, and they knew I was drinking. They all looked at me and thought, *Poor Jessie. With all she's been through, it's understandable.*

But I knew my drinking was getting destructive. I was starting to wake up in the morning and barf my brains out—and look in the mirror and think, *What am I becoming? What am I turning into?* One morning, I woke up at ten when I was supposed to lead a meeting at nine, and I thought, *I just can't do this anymore.*

I knew if I called my parents in New Hampshire and said, "I've got a problem with alcohol," there would be no backing out. If they knew I was in trouble, I would have to do something about it. So that's what I did—I got Mom and Dad on the phone, and both of them were crying. And my dad got on a plane and flew out, and that was the start of trying to save my life.

I entered a good treatment center, and I didn't have a problem at all with the first step. My behavior had been such that believing I was an alcoholic was not a problem, and my life was certainly unmanageable. But they encouraged me to go to AA after discharge, and I had a hard time visualizing AA being a part of my life. I was still doing the "terminally unique" routine 'cause I was proud of the fact that in treatment people would mistake me for a staff member. So even though I was talking all the right stuff, I was thinking, *I'm not the same as these people*—I'm not. *I'm smarter, you know.*

After treatment, I didn't get a sponsor for months because I needed to interview the right kind of person. I also wasn't keen on the idea that I needed somebody to explain this stuff to me—it made perfect sense, and I didn't see why I needed that much guidance.

Plus my first AA meeting scared the shit out of me. It was during lunch, and I went completely across town because I didn't want to run into anybody I knew. So I ended up at this biker meeting in a pink linen suit. Talk about standing out! Everybody at the meeting, including the women, had tattoos. It was just bizarre.

And the guy chairing the meeting looked scary as hell. He was massive, wore his biker jacket, and had a mane of salt-and-pepper hair with a large beard. He stared at me, standing there with my blonde hair in my little pink suit, and said, "If you're new in this room and this is your first AA meeting, I promise you that AA has fucked up your drinking—forever." The man scared me to death.

Of course, I could say then, "I'm not like these people . . . I'm not like these people."

At a different AA meeting, all they talked about was "God, God."

*What the hell does any of this have to do with alcohol and trying to stop drinking?* I thought. It didn't seem like anything they said had to do with not drinking. Of course, I didn't introduce myself as a newcomer, so nobody had reason to focus on issues that arise when you're just getting sober.

I also considered myself pretty much an atheist, thinking God was made up by man as a way of dealing with life's tragedies. So when people talked about God, I reacted with, "What the fuck is this about?" And out the door I went, thinking, *This isn't for me.*

Treatment had made far more sense because they got into some of the scientific facts of alcoholism. But when they told me that I had to go to AA, and that it was a spiritual solution, I told them I would have a real problem with it.

I didn't buy that part in the Big Book where it says "knowledge is not enough." I thought if I knew enough about this, knew how dangerous it was, and knew what kind of shape it had gotten me into before, then *of course* I was not going to drink again.

I thought that as long as I didn't drink, everything would be perfect. There wasn't a whole lot more to it than that.

And guess what? I relapsed.


Soon after I got out of treatment, I got a job offer from a different company to move up to Santa Clara. And just in the nick of time because, boy, my employer was ready to boot my ass out the door, real fast. My boss treated me like a criminal. And then an international company stepped in and said, "We want you to come work for us in Santa Clara." I was so relieved to get out. And my new employer has been incredibly good to me.

When I moved to my new job, I didn't go to many meetings. I'd gone sporadically in Los Angeles, even though I had doubts about their efficacy. But when I got to Santa Clara, they didn't even run the meetings exactly the same way, and I wasn't comfortable with that—so I stopped going.

Six weeks later, I was sent to a month-long training at corporate headquarters in New York. The last night there, I was flirting with this tall, gorgeous guy, and my boss was telling me how everyone at the training thought I was the best and brightest.

We're all dressed up for this banquet, and Mr. Gorgeous is telling me how fabulous I look, and I'm just thinking, *Damn, I'm good!* Damn, *I'm good!* Then the waitress comes around for drink orders. My heart is just beating as she makes her way around the table, and this voice is telling me, "You're gonna fuck it up. You're gonna fuck it up." But another is saying, "You've got it wrapped, lady. The job's going great, and there's this wonderful guy you're going to sleep with tonight." Then the clincher: "You're in control—*it was because of the divorce.*"

So when the waitress gets to me, I hear myself saying, "Tanqueray and tonic."

When I got back in the program, I read chapter three in the Big Book, and it pissed me off that I was such a textbook relapse case.

Everything in there was me—trying to be terminally unique, attempting to make myself different from others who had become addicted, not going to meetings, not talking to a sponsor. I walked directly into it, doing exactly what it said I would, and all the knowledge about how bad it could be didn't make a bit of difference.

The night of the banquet, I drank moderately and thought later, *Well, nothing bad happened. In fact, some good things happened.* So I drank on the plane on the way home, and within two weeks, I was drinking as usual, sitting on the couch at night with my remote control.

Finally, I called a treatment center and went to a night program for a few days to get back on track. I stayed sober for a couple of months, but the old mind got to working again, telling me, *It wasn't all that bad.* Then I had a conversation with a friend who said, "Well, I sort of think I'm probably an alcoholic, but I look at drinking—or drinking too much—like cheating on a diet." And I really liked that analogy. "Yeah, I'll just blow off my no-alcohol diet for a couple of weeks," he said, "and then I'll go to meetings again and control my drinking with AA."

When I tried that, it didn't work. I worked sales out of my house again and was supposed to be in the field. Even though all my customers were in the same town, I didn't call on them in person. Instead, I drank and dealt with them over the phone. When I had a meeting to attend at our office, I got cleaned up, went to work, and did what I needed to do. But the minute I had a chance to start drinking again, that's what I did. At night I'd sometimes drink to the point where I'd wake up in the middle of my apartment. The next morning I would see evidence in the bathroom that indicated I had taken a bath, but I didn't remember it at all. *I'm gonna end up dead,* I thought.

That progressed to where I was just not able to do much of anything. There were weeks at a time when I didn't go out of my apartment except to buy booze. Really! And, man, my apartment looked *horrible.* It was a reflection of me—it was trashed.

My old sponsor kept trying to get in touch with me, but I wouldn't return her calls. My boss I kept at bay by returning some of his, but toward the end he was hassling me because I wasn't even checking my voice mail. And I certainly wasn't going outside to get the regular mail—that just seemed like too much trouble. I had money in the bank, but I wasn't writing the checks to pay my bills. That was too much to do.

When I went home for Christmas, my family knew I was drinking, and they were afraid. When I got back on the plane, Dad was crying because he thought he might never see me again.

I had talked with my sister one night, telling her how much better it would be for everybody if I wasn't around. One of my men friends had tried to talk me into buying a gun for protection. He's a good old country boy and his solution to everything is to have a gun in the house. *If I have a gun here,* I remember thinking, *I'll get loaded one night and blow my brains out.* But I really did wish I were dead and desired some peaceful way to die, either by drinking enough or just not waking up in the morning. I could not stop drinking, and having heard enough about recovery, I thought I was one of those alcoholics who would never get it. I was going to die young, and I was going to die a drunk.

I remember driving home after an appointment and going through withdrawals. It was like alcohol was oozing out of me, and me thinking, *Don't stop at the liquor store, don't stop at the liquor store, don't stop at the liquor store. Just go home, just go home, just go home.* But I had to stop at the store—and started crying. And going home and pouring the Tanqueray in the glass, crying because I knew I had to, even though I didn't want to.

I tried going back to some AA meetings, but I'd only go home and get loaded again. I went to big meetings, where it's easy to get lost in the crowd; and I didn't talk, so nobody knew me, and no one could help me. Finally, in January, I decided I needed to step away from work and everything else—I felt I needed to be locked up for a little while.

So I called home and said, "I've got to try treatment again."

Dad flew out, and I had a hard time just getting to the airport to pick him up, because it was everything I could do to get there. I felt like I couldn't function. I couldn't move. I couldn't eat. I couldn't do anything but drink.

When my father came into the apartment, I just crawled onto the couch, and he looked around my once-gorgeous apartment with its high ceilings and started crying. He got on the phone and I heard him say, "This is an emergency."

Dad helped me get into the Good Samaritan Recovery Center in San Jose. Now I was at the point where my attitude was, "Just tell me what it is I have to do, and I'll do it." I was so friggin' willing. It was where I had to be, you know.

I was in that wonderful place for twenty-four days, and then in a seven-week relapse-prevention program that met four nights a week. And I started doing AA in a big way because I was so afraid of going back to where I was.

And AA had changed. There were still people who looked very different from me, but now they said things that made sense and made me realize that we were alike in many ways. There were also meetings where I made friends with people doing the same kind of work. And women I'd want to hang out with, going shopping or eating. I'd never seen any of those people, in part because they weren't at the meetings I went to, but mainly because I didn't *want* to see them. Judgment had put scales over my eyes. When I became more willing, I was able to see that I had something in common with everybody in those rooms. I didn't have to be friends with them all, but I became very good friends with some.

To my great surprise, after treatment I got a review of my past work, and my boss gave me an excellent review. Amazingly, the sales numbers were there—the charts showed me to be at 150 percent of my goal. Part of that was luck, but I'd also somehow managed, by doing the bare minimum, to keep going what was needed.

During treatment, my boss had been wonderful. He sent me flowers, saying, "We miss you. Can't wait until you're back!" The difference was like night and day when I got out of treatment the second time. Employers can do two things that don't work—they can either treat you like a criminal, or they can coddle you so much that they stress you out while simultaneously not allowing you to do your job. My boss simply handed me the files and said, "Glad you're back!"

I will always be grateful to that man. At the beginning, I told him I needed to take a month off under a doctor's care because I was sick from drinking a whole lot. I didn't want the word "alco-holism" in my file, so I let him know without spelling it out, so that he wouldn't have to put it in there.

"If you bring me a doctor's note that you're under his care," he said, "you've got the time with full pay. If not, you can take a month off—no questions asked. As far as I'm concerned, it's like you've got a broken leg." And that's exactly how he behaved.

He's a wonderful man. I had two broken legs, coupla broken arms, you know.

More recently, a territory opened in another state, and I chose to take it, even though I was afraid. Here I was moving to a new town again with new AA and everything else. I was petrified of relapsing again because I absolutely believe that if I get drunk again, I'm going to end up dead.

But this move was so different for me because now I bought the idea that you take away what sounds good for you and leave the rest. In other words, I was more open to hearing what worked. And in spite of myself and regardless of all my analyses, I somehow found God in this program. It still blows me away that that happened, because I was so sure that He did not exist.

For a while, I did use the group as my Higher Power because I could concede that this whole bunch of people staying sober was much stronger than anything I had managed on my own. But in doing this program, getting a sponsor, and trying to work the steps, I somehow found God and have a faith today that I didn't think was possible. And my life is so incredibly different now. I don't have a thing to complain about. My problems today, as we say, are high-class problems.

When I moved, my family thought it was a horrible decision. I didn't know anybody, I didn't have a support system, and I was going to get drunk. But something about it felt right from the beginning, and that has continued. It has felt right because I asked for help as soon as I got here, and I got connected real quickly. The fact that I was scared caused me to reach out like never before. As a result, I have been rewarded with people in my life who totally love me and would be there for absolutely anything.

I made a point of staying after meetings, so I could join people who were going for lunch or coffee. I wasn't always with a crowd I felt comfortable in, and sometimes I just wanted to get out of there, but it got me to meet some good people. And it got me recognized, so that when I was out of town traveling for a couple of weeks, I'd come back and they would say, "Gosh, it's really good to see you! I've missed you!" And that felt great.

And whenever there was some activity going on, such as planning for a dance or party, I made sure I was a part of that. I feel so connected today that I can walk into any AA room in the world and feel perfectly comfortable. AA just feels like home to me.

But when I walk up to a meeting at my home group and into that room, it's like a sanctuary to me. No matter what's going on in my life, I can sit down and start feeling better. And I know that the people there really care about me, and that's a wonderful feeling. I've got a very close and loving family, and they would do anything for me, but they don't *understand* me at all. None of them are alcoholics. So my home group's a special place for me—people love me *and* understand me.

When I was first trying to get sober, I remember a sponsor telling me, "If you keep sobriety as your first priority, and if you work the steps to this program, all of the other stuff will just fall into place." And that has been true for me.

Today, I am truly happy, and I always thought that would never happen. I believed that I was one of those people who was destined to have miserable things happen all the time. That there was something about me that meant I was going to be unhappy, and that was just the way my life would be.

I see so much hope in everything! I used to think there wasn't anyone more despicable, and that I was a pretty pathetic excuse for a woman. Now my sense of self-respect and self-esteem is vibrant. It's integrated into knowing that I am a blessed child of God and nobody can take that away from me. The only thing that can take that away from me today is taking another drink.

I also know today that when I get away from meetings for a week at a time, I start getting nuts. I believe in the analogy between alcoholism and diabetes. If you're a diabetic and don't take the insulin, you start getting sick. And if I get away from meetings, my priorities shift, and the bullshit starts taking over a bigger place in my brain, whether it's about work or family or relationships. I begin magnifying silly things, which makes me anxious and tense. And then, after a period of time, I'll start thinking about alcohol again. Not in the sense that I want to get drunk, but romanticizing, "Oh, yeah, wouldn't it be nice to have a glass of wine with dinner." That usually doesn't happen when I'm going to meetings regularly.

For somebody whose every waking thought was around alcohol, it's an absolute miracle that I go through most days without thinking about it at all. And that just blows my mind! I'm always put in situations where alcohol is a part of life. But when I'm going to meetings, it's very easy to say, "Club soda." That's automatic. My response to stress today is not, "Gosh, I need a drink." My response to stress today is, "Gosh, I need a meeting."

That's what works for me. My sister, who's not an alcoholic, was here this weekend, and I took her to a meeting. Trying to explain to her how it works is impossible. She was like, "I don't get it. Why is it you say that if you don't go to meetings, you start thinking differently?"

"I don't know, but I do."

When I'm in the meetings and I'm talking about what's going on for me, not necessarily about drinking or anything, but when I'm speaking and participating in my own sobriety, I do OK. And when I don't go to meetings, it appears that alcoholism is like this little demon inside of me, waiting for an opportunity to get hold of my brain. Really! Because it just does amazing things. My brain is a bizarre place, you know, and when I'm not going to meetings, the alcoholic side of my brain starts getting a handle on me. And that's a real dangerous place for me to be.

I get into profound gratitude whenever I start thinking about AA because it's my lifeline. And I never thought spirituality would be a significant part of my life. Yet today, I can't get enough of it. I'm also doing more as far as getting involved in church, and I'm taking a meditation class because I believe that God is inside me and everybody else, and I'm still trying to learn how to tap into that. I've had moments since I've been sober where I have felt really connected to God. When I do, I wonder what else I can do to make that happen more often.

I've been blessed with a sponsor for whom I have a tremendous amount of love and respect. Without saying a word, she somehow guides me to what I need to do for me.

And I've gotten much better about setting boundaries with people and knowing what's good for me and what's not, and what I'm willing to put up with and what not. There's a whole lot I'm not willing to put up with today. And I'm much better about making that clear.

My friends are real different now, and they are great. My closest friends are Carol, who's sixty-three, and Cheryl, who just turned thirty and at times is real childlike. Then I have a whole group of friends I can socialize with and talk to whenever I need. Socially, I've got more going on than ever.

I built a beautiful home, which is very symbolic to me of getting my life back in order. Between the financial difficulties generated by the marriage and those caused by my own drinking and irresponsible behavior, my credit was just horrible. So when I moved into my home, I felt at peace in the realization that things are starting to work for me.

Although it's only been two years, usually my drinking seems a lifetime ago. At other times, just talking about it, I can feel how intensely miserable I was back then. And it couldn't be more of a dichotomy—to look at where I was then and where I am now, it's two completely different people.

There are two entirely separate worlds happening simultaneously, and some people who are where I used to be don't have a clue that the other world is there for the asking at all times. When I found it, I thought I was the kind of alcoholic who had tried it, and it didn't work. And I hear people say that now, and I think, *Oh, God, what didn't work? Who didn't work?*

# 19

## MICHELLE

I passed my childhood in a moving bubble. All the kids seemed to be having fun, whether at a birthday party or on the playground—but there was something wrong with me.

It makes sense. My brother and I were both in diapers when Grandpa died and Dad excused himself to go run the family business. Then my sister popped out, and Mom had no time for us either.

Dad's drinking problem became obvious as I grew older. When he came home, I was always excited to see him, but I never knew what mood he would be in—whether full of rage or real gooey.

During my teenage years, Mom was always depressed, and Dad would tell us, "Don't make waves. Help your mother out." I had to stop being a child and started raising my sister. As I got into adolescence and my body began changing, Mom was no help because she couldn't even say the word "sick," much less talk about menstruation. I was worried, not knowing what was happening, but Mother was too embarrassed to set me at ease. Between my drunk father and depressed, uncommunicative mother, my childhood was dreadful.

We sipped Dad's beer as early as I can remember. But the first time I drank on my own was in eighth grade at a neighbor's house. I felt weird at school the next day because it was a religious institution where I made straight As in Bible class. I could tell you who begat whom and knew the stories by heart, but I had no sense of spirituality, prayer, meditation, or a personal God. Nothing. But when I had that first drink, *I knew I had found it.*

I was a jock, starting on the varsity basketball team as a sophomore, and a tomboy who participated in everything, whether flag football, baseball, or waterskiing. I even rode my own six-foot-tall unicycle powered by a long chain.

I partied throughout high school, with widely varying results. Sometimes I'd be the life of the party, running around loving everybody, dancing, and having a great time. At other times, I'd be mean and cuss out my little sister. Once, I even ended up sitting in a car with my girlfriends, crying. I couldn't talk. I just bawled—and had no idea why.

The tears surprised me. Mom was always depressed and crying, acting like a dumb little doormat, and there was no way I was going to be a weakling like her. I was strong and independent, and crying was stupid. But sometimes I could only find out what was going on inside me by getting so drunk that I cracked my exterior shell. But I never knew what I would find underneath, whether I was going to be happy, or sad, or so angry that I'd try to punch somebody out.

The main reason I drank was that I felt less comfortable sober. It wasn't conscious, but I just wanted relief from my feelings. And when I got drunk, the alcohol brought etherized serenity.

The morning following another crying episode, a friend asked, "Do you *remember* what you were saying last night?" I got that sinking feeling in the pit of my stomach and thought, *Oh, my God . . . what did I say?*

"You were sobbing, saying that you felt completely alone and empty inside." And that was exactly right—the loneliness was awful, and I didn't know what to do about it.

My senior year in high school, I became so petrified about leaving home and going to college that I developed an eating disorder. I was afraid when I wasn't supposed to be, and I didn't know how to deal with it, so I drank a lot and didn't eat much. That has haunted me since.

When I actually got to college, I loved it from the moment I stepped on campus. We had a thousand students on enchanting grounds. I hooked up with a great group of friends and joined a wonderful sorority.

We all partied, of course—any occasion was an excuse to drink.

But for the first time, somebody confronted me about my drinking. The morning after one party, a sorority sister said, "Michelle, I love you to death and I don't want to lose your friendship, but you drank too much last night, and the truth is you do that too often." And when we'd be out drinking together, she'd say, "Drink a glass of water before ordering another one."

Occasionally, I would think that something was fundamentally wrong with my drinking. But I wasn't ready to do anything about it. I would also blame it on my frustration in not being able to settle on a major or find the right person to date. *If I can just get my life straightened out,* I'd think, *I wouldn't drink like this.* I read self-help books for answers and decided that I just needed to think positive. Just be positive. Don't be negative.

The summer following my freshman year, we had a blowup on our family vacation when Dad got drunk and blasted my brother in front of everybody, including my brother's best friend. Humiliated, my brother got in his car and left. The rest of us, including his friend, drove home the next day, acting as if nothing was wrong.

I knew my brother had probably gone to his girlfriend's house in another state. As soon as we got home, I surreptitiously called there. When I was talking to him, Dad walked in, got on the phone, and said, "I'm sorry. I was wrong." I was glad to be sitting; otherwise, I probably would have fallen down. Admitting error was not in our family lexicon.

Then Dad took me out on the porch and gave me a speech about careers in accounting. I was the obedient child. He would never tell me what to do; just say what he thought, and expect me to be the good girl I'd always been and follow suit.

In the fall, I started taking all these accounting classes and just hated them. I felt compelled to continue and couldn't see a way out, so I began playing this little control game. I would see how little I could eat and how long I could fast. When big things happened that I couldn't control, I rebelled by controlling my body.

In the meantime, I played first-team varsity college basketball, starting from our opening game my freshman year through my last game as a senior. By my sophomore year, however, I was drinking twice as much and eating half of what I should. Because of that combination, a friend had to help me walk out of TGI Friday's in Louisville one night, which had never happened before. I could always hold my liquor and could walk and drive just fine.

That Christmas, I went home very thin, but continued to party. At one gathering, I was drinking my usual white wine, grazing on cheese balls, when they ran out of white. So what the hell, I drank red, even though I hated it.

The next morning I woke up to a spinning room, ran into the bathroom with the pressure coming up my throat—and vomited all over the sink. Then I fell down to my knees, stuck my head in the commode, and puked again.

"Oh, my God! What's wrong, honey?" my mother asked, as she put her hands on my shoulders.

"Wwwwrrrretttch!" I replied, with involuntary tears popping out of my eyes from the acid in my nostrils, and pieces of green food splattering all over the white ceramic bowl.

"Let me get you some water," Mom said, hurrying away. When she came back, I felt a cool, wet washcloth press against my neck. I took a sip from a glass of water between retches.

"Are you all right, honey?"

"I don't know. I ate some cheese balls last night."

The thought of food triggered still another round of painful vomiting, with nothing but clear digestive fluid coming up. I felt as if I were trying to turn my stomach inside-out past my teeth.

Dad came in to help. We tried water, soda, Alka-Seltzer . . .

An hour-and-a-half later, my worried parents rushed me to the Emergency Room, with me in a state of exhaustion, but still making excruciating heaving sounds into a towel in the backseat, with nothing coming out of my mouth.

At the hospital, they immediately fed me intravenously to get my body chemistry back to a semblance of balance. The hospital chart read "Dehydration."

Two hours later, the doctor came in for his final check. "How are you feeling, young lady?"

"Fine, now. I must have eaten something bad."

He hesitated, tilted his head forward, stared at me over his glasses, and sternly warned, "You're going to have to stay away from alcohol."

The following week, I was back at basketball practice—which was a total joke, me walking into the gym. The trainer looked at me like I'd lost my mind. I thought that since I could walk around, I was perfectly OK.

My first three years in college, I drank less during basketball season, and not at all the night before a game. But by the time my senior year rolled around, I was drinking almost every night. We had no written training rules, such as "No drinking during the season." (But that became one after I left.)

One Saturday, we played Indiana on the road, and our team performed so poorly that Coach didn't even bother to come down after the game to cuss us out. We were all bummed, so I suggested that we should party when we got back to Louisville. I called ahead for somebody to go to the liquor store, since we wouldn't get back until three o'clock Sunday morning. Once back at the dorm, we sat around, got drunk, and talked about what a bitch Coach was.

On Monday, I had a couple of drinks during lunch with a friend, which led to an afternoon of barhopping. When practice began at 5:30, I blew in totally trashed. Ordinarily, I was intense and made the highest scores in our shooting drills. But now it didn't matter. When I missed, I fell down at Coach's feet, laughing hysterically.

"I just have one thing to say," Coach barked after practice, as she lined us up for running drills. "If you come to practice, you better come ready to play . . . and if you're not ready to play, don't *bother* showing up."

By that time I had sobered up a little and knew it was directed at me. After practice I went up to her and said, "I think we need to talk."

"Come into my office." She pointed at the door, stormed in, and sat down behind her desk in disgust.

"Coach, I didn't mean for this to happen. I had wine with lunch and then one thing just led to another. I'm *really* sorry."

She sat for a long time, staring pensively into space. Finally, she looked at me and said, "Michelle, you're a good ballplayer, but I often wonder why you go to such extremes at whatever you do. Have you ever thought about going to counseling?"

So I started seeing a psychologist Coach knew. We talked all about my childhood, but he never said anything about my drinking, so I inferred that it was OK for me to drink.

I still suspected that I had some defect that drove me to medicate my feelings, and if I could only learn what was wrong with me and correct it, I wouldn't drink like I did. I hoped therapy would help me find the solution, but it never did.


Close to graduation, I thought, *When I get out of school and go back home, I'll settle down.*

Once there, though, I picked up right where I left off in college, drinking the same old way. I blamed it on my fear of the future, because I had no idea what I wanted to do. *When I get a job, I'll clean up my act* was my next rationale.

But when I finally got a bank job in November, I was still drinking. That I blamed on Dad's humongous bar. So I decided, *I'll quit when I move out of the house. I just won't keep alcohol at my place.*

So I got a condo, which turned out to be a mile from this big liquor warehouse. I'd find myself in the car, going there—not wanting to go there—knowing what was going to happen, but thinking it would be different this time.

By now it was a constant battle trying to control my drinking. Many times I would think, *I've got a drinking problem,* only to be followed the next day by, *What a silly thought!* That weekend, I'd decide, *I do have a drinking problem.* But by Wednesday, it was, *That was so stupid!*

In the meantime, Mom started going to Al-Anon because of Dad's drinking and her own depression, and she began having a ball and doing great. One day Mom mentioned that a girl from my high school had spoken to her group about alcoholism, her own recovery, and her experiences with her dad being an alcoholic. Missy was the most beautiful girl in our school—cheerleader, homecoming queen, her dad was a doctor . . . She had it made, you know? Perfect on the outside.

Mom commented, "If you ever see Missy, you might want to talk to her." Boy, talk about making me jump!

*Oh, God! . . . Mom knows,* I thought. But Mom was clueless. She meant that I should talk to Missy about having an alcoholic father.

Within six weeks of moving into my own place, the Kentucky Derby came to town. It's a huge event, where half the gambling spectators have never even *seen* a horse. My college friends came up for a reunion, including one guy who was like a brother to me, having watched out for me in college.

After the race, both of us got drunk and went off to dinner at this girl's house. My buddy had this joint hidden behind his ear that we were going to smoke if certain people would leave. But they never would, and that pissed us off. So we went to my condo, sat on the deck, and took only three hits apiece because the pot was so strong. Then we walked down to the river and sat on the bank, mesmerized by the black, watery canvas, which was splashed with bursts of sparkling city lights.

After a few minutes, which seemed like an eternity because of the pot, my friend leaned over and kissed me. "What are you *doing?*" I recoiled. But he put his arm around me and tried to continue.

"I can't handle this!" I said, scrambling to my feet. "Let's go!"

He spent the night at my house as planned, which originally had been no big deal. But now he snuck into my bed in the middle of the night.

"Don't touch me!"

"Oh, come on, Michelle."

"We're just friends, Arnie, and I want to keep it that way."

"But you feel so good . . ."

"No, don't *do* that!"

In my intoxicated stupor, I fought him all night long, because I just wasn't attracted to this guy. I woke up exhausted the next morning, and thought, *What the hell's wrong with me? How did I get myself into this? My world's a mess. I've got to do* something.

I felt horrible . . . confused . . . hung over . . . and hit rock bottom.


I called Mom from work that day and got Missy's phone number, thinking, *Maybe there's a solution here.* But when I came home from the bank that evening, I started cleaning my condo. *If I just get busy,* I thought, *this idea will go away, like it usually does.* So I washed the dishes, vacuumed the house, dusted the corners and windowsills, cleaned the bathtubs, scrubbed the toilets, mopped the floors. But the thought would *not* go away.

So I called Missy and said, "I need to talk to you."

The next night, this pretty young girl sat in my living room and told me the history of her feelings and drinking. She put my insides in words, which was an absolute miracle! I mean, it was all the gut stuff that I had been feeling for years.

She took me to my first AA meeting. And I've been going ever since—sort of. You know, I had to try it my way first by only going to a few meetings, not reaching out to people, and refusing to get a sponsor. Once I became miserable enough, I ended up in treatment.

I wanted somebody to fix me without me having to do anything. I wanted treatment to be like a Laundromat: stick me in a machine, churn me around, fix me up nice and perfect, fold me, and send me out in the world to live happily ever after.

And that didn't happen.

As the years went by, I drifted away and became depressed again. But I'd go to a meeting once in a while just to say I was going. At five years' sober, I bought a new car to celebrate, and that feel-good fix lasted about a week.

Eventually I got so miserable that I went to counseling, which helped tremendously. I also began attending three or four meetings a week—showing up early, talking to people, and going for coffee afterwards. At last, I got a sponsor, worked the steps, and began sponsoring other women.

One of my neatest discoveries in this, my seventh year, is a spiritual bond. Last winter I was depressed and struggling, going to meetings every day—trying so *hard.* And I journaled my yearning for the spiritual connection that all these other people seemed to have, and how empty I felt not having it.

Over the course of the year, I've done some things differently, including going to codependency treatment, and that's been a blessing, especially in teaching me to be true to myself. Now I feel that I have a good base for a spiritual connection with a God of my understanding. It just blows me away that within a year of putting one foot in front of the other and taking suggestions, it just *happened.*

It's not perfect and I want it to grow, but that's been the big gift this year. I want to be an instrument of God's love and peace. That's where it's at.


I've always been talented athletically, and I threw much of that away because I had a bad attitude that resulted indirectly from drinking. In college, I scored 32 points in one game, shooting 80 percent from the field. Then I thought, *The next game I'm going to score 40 points and be 100 percent from the field.* When I missed my first three shots in that one, I said, "Fuck this, I'm not gonna shoot." Of course, Coach took me out and didn't play me the rest of the game. And then *she* was the bitch.

But it was "me, me, me," you know. If I had a bad game and we won, I pouted. If I had a good game and we lost, I was in a great mood. I was ranked nationally in field-goal percentage as a freshman until I discovered that fact. Then I put pressure on myself to make the paper every week and screwed up my game.

I've played in a few leagues since I've been sober, and I'm no longer so self-absorbed. I actually laugh at myself now.

Coaching young girls' teams has presented some eerie experiences. One year I coached a girl whose attitude reminded me so much of me. Nothing was ever good enough. After she'd make five shots in a row, she was on top of the world. But when she missed the next five, she'd get visibly upset and depressed and want to quit basketball. I shook my head and thought, *Oh, God, please, please help her.*

I'd put money on the fact that she's out there medicating.


Looking back, I can see now that my eating disorder and drinking went hand in hand. Sometimes I'd drink at night instead of eat. Then the next day I wouldn't be hungry because I felt sick from drinking. Both fasting and drinking also gave me a high—there's an intoxicating euphoria in being able to stay so thin. And both created a wall between me and other people. Fasting was a subconscious effort to stay separate; and though drinking begins as a social lubricant, it actually produces separation because it functions as an escape from the reality of the moment and true relationship. Also, having the willpower to eat little or nothing made me feel powerful and in control, the same "bulletproof" feeling I got from alcohol.

The cure for both was to admit powerlessness and ask for help.

One of the ways I limited my eating was by running. I was a *runner,* not a jogger, and I would run *at* myself—running eight miles, not only because I wanted to, but because I *had* to. There's a euphoria with that, from the endorphins, which helped me run away from myself and deaden the pain.

Drinking, fasting, and running—all worked to numb and escape the dull, chronic pain in my gut. I thought I was supposed to be able to handle it alone, and I never wanted to admit weakness. But all I was doing was postponing a life of peace and freedom.

# 20

## SARAH BETH

O ne day I decided that I wanted life to be radically different. I wanted *everything* to change. So I headed out west to open a new business. I got a break from my husband, quit my job, and changed cities—all at the same time.

I grew up in Baton Rouge, Louisiana, and had never lived anyplace else. So at age forty-seven, with grown children and a perfectly good husband, I moved to a restored mining town on the side of a mountain in Nevada.

I got out there and discovered that I didn't have a problem with life—I had a problem with drinking. And it was painful.

I'd never had a drink before I was twenty-seven. At the time, I was a successful interior designer and my husband was a stockbroker. We went to Mexico with several couples, and they all drank tequila (they called it "ta-kill-ya") with lime and salt. They drank a lot and had great fun, while I ran around with them, not drinking, feeling inhibited.

When we came home and had a party, I decided to drink "ta-kill-ya" with them. And, of course, I got drunk. I look back now and realize that all I needed to do was take a drink. Once I started drinking alcohol, I wanted more. The only difference between me and them was I *wanted* to get drunk. Occasionally, they'd talk about party events that I couldn't remember, and I thought I was in the other room when they happened. Now I recognize that I must have been out of the room a lot.

After the first night, I realized it wasn't time for me to party. I had young children and didn't want to drink my life away, so I indulged rarely. But every time I did, I kept going till I was drunk. And I suffered terrible hangovers.

While the kids were at home, my drinking during the year was limited to the occasional dinner party we had in each other's homes, where everybody would drink, and eat, and dance. We did attend a number of holiday parties, however, with many of my hangovers occurring around Christmastime.

After the children were grown, I was in my early forties and started "controlled" drinking. I thought if I practiced control, that's all it would take. So I allowed myself two drinks. But eventually it got to where the first two drinks would make me tipsy, and I wouldn't care what I drank after that. For some reason, alcohol severely affected my body. It was painful, and it wasn't pretty, but I drank it anyway.

For several years I realized that I wasn't drinking the way others did, or it wasn't affecting me the way it did them. But I never thought I was an alcoholic because I never drank during the day, I didn't drink every night, and I would go for long periods without having anything. But when I did, I just didn't like the way I drank or how I felt afterward. And I kept trying to find a way to drink normally.

"God, help me control my drinking," I used to pray, and for a while I wouldn't have a problem with it.

When I decided to move to Nevada by myself, my husband of thirty years was supportive, which is something that a man in a normal marriage would never do. But looking back, there wasn't anything normal about the way we did things anymore.

On arriving in Nevada, I was away from everybody I knew and, to my surprise, started drinking regularly. I'd close up my business at the end of the day and go have my first drink. What bothered me was that there was no reason for that. I was my own boss and was living alone, doing exactly what I wanted for the first time in my life, and yet I couldn't stop this habit. Within months, I drank nearly every night, and there was no getting around it anymore—I *had* to drink virtually every night.

I'd look in the mirror in the morning and hate what I was seeing. It was breaking my heart. And I was so embarrassed because I'd seen people who were drunk, and I despised that.

*When I go home for the fall,* I thought, *I'll be OK around my old support system and the people I love, and my drinking will get better.*

But a month after I returned to Louisiana, my drinking was even worse.

One night, I fell to my knees and prayed to God to help me stop drinking. For once, I didn't ask, "Please help me control it." Instead, I implored, *"Please* help me, Father! I want this *out of my life!"*

The next morning all I could think of was calling Judy, a woman I hadn't spoken to in two years. In our last conversation, she'd been so obnoxious that I'd decided never to call her again. *God, I don't want to call her,* I thought. *She's the worst drunk I know.* But I just felt compelled to talk with her.

When I reached Judy, she was so nice that it surprised me. She said to meet her about nine o'clock that night. "Why so late?" I asked.

"I have something to do, and I'll meet you afterward."

We met at a restaurant and she looked wonderful—sparkly eyed and happy. I had a glass of wine, and Judy ordered a sandwich and milk. After eating, she said, "Let's go to your house and visit some more. It's really nice to see you."

At my home, I opened the bar and Judy got a 7UP. We talked until two, and I was mesmerized by her joy and excitement. At one point, I got up for a refill and asked, "Would you like a *real* drink?"

"No, thanks," she said, "I'm chemically free." And that's all she mentioned.

After she left, I thought, *My, God, if Judy knows how not to drink, there's hope for me. If she can do that and she knows the key, I want to know it, too.*

———

The following weekend was my typical form of private hell, so I called Judy first thing Monday morning, and mumbled, "I need to talk to you about a problem."

"What is it?"

"I want to quit drinking, and it looks like you know how *not* to drink."

"OK, Sarah Beth, why don't we get together and talk about that tonight? I'll pick you up at seven-thirty, if that's all right. In the meantime, try not to drink today. Do whatever you have to, but don't drink any more than is absolutely necessary."

When I climbed into Judy's car that night, a guy was in the backseat, and I noticed that he wore a full beard and an earring. I was miffed. Why did she bring this man with her when I wanted to talk to her about my secret problem? After fifteen minutes of riding along in silence, we pulled up in front of this little house.

"What are we doing *here?*" I asked.

Judy smiled and took my hand. "We're going to take you in to meet some people who'll love you like you've *never* been loved before," she said.

"What *is* this, an AA meeting?"

"Yeah, that's the best place I know for us."


The poor woman chairing the meeting stopped halfway through and said to a guy, "Big Mike, I just can't do this. Would you take this meeting and chair it?" I didn't understand what was happening. I had no idea that I was being disruptive, continually interjecting questions, because I was the center of the universe.

Mike must have been gentle with me because, somehow or other, I got the message that I needed to listen. If he'd been belligerent or factual—"You sit there and hush and listen!"—I probably would have walked out because I was arrogant. I knew better than any of those people. *My word!*

Before the end of the meeting, enough love was in that room that it completely changed the way I felt—just like it does in most meetings. I usually can't sit there without eventually knowing that I'm connected with a love I didn't come in with. (In fact, I called God "Love" for years because I couldn't say "God." I realized after a while that I didn't know what love was either, but I could at least say the word.)

When I found a way out that night, I was so relieved and grateful. But sobriety has not been particularly easy.

At first, I was antagonistic toward spirituality. And, big surprise, I was also reluctant to make essential changes. Of course, life has changed. For one, I never dreamed that I would ever be divorced. I'd been married since I was seventeen, a total of thirty-two years when John and I called it quits, and I never imagined that would happen—or that it would be OK.

It took about a year of sobriety to recognize that my life and my marriage were a mess. I had totally ignored that, just drank it away, unwilling to look at anything I was doing. I thought if I made enough money as an interior designer and everything looked good, life had to be OK. Naturally, after I got sober, I realized that this wasn't acceptable behavior at all.

John didn't quit drinking. He still hasn't. When I look at him today, my heart just breaks. He remarried a year or two after our divorce and got himself another enabling lady. She's about twenty years younger and a nurse, and every time he gets sick, she takes him to the hospital, where they run yet another test. But he doesn't get better. The kids, of course, say, "God, Dad, why don't you go to AA?"

For a long time we had vacationed in a cabin along a Louisiana riverbank. At a year sober, I spent the summer there and went to my first AA meeting in a country town. Eleven men attended AA. They met once a week, and there were no women. The wives called themselves Al-Anon wives, and they were not at the first meeting I went to, but believe me, they were at the second. They had heard from their husbands that a *woman* came to AA.

I was quite the novelty!

The men were pleased to have me attend because no woman had ever come. It wasn't as if no women needed it, they just wouldn't come out. I found out why when a woman who was "new" in town—she had lived there for *seven years!*—invited me to the monthly luncheon of all churchwomen in the area. The event was on the first Monday of the month, and I met many women who were active in the community and several of the ministers' wives. I was so delighted to make some women friends.

The next day I saw the woman who had invited me to the luncheon at one of the three local restaurants, and she acted like she'd never seen me before. *How strange!* I thought. Then I went to wash my car, and one of the ministers' wives was there with her little girl. I drove into the car wash, got out, and started talking to her. She immediately grabbed her little girl, put her in the car, and drove off—*with soap all over her car!*

I searched out one of the guys, an old man who'd been the local iceman and had been sober for twenty-seven years. "You're gonna run into problems here," he had warned me, "and you'll need people to talk to. I want you to know that you can talk to me."

So I went to him and asked, *"What's* going *on?"*

"Sarah Beth, you're in a small town, and when you go to church on Sunday, everybody knows which church you attend. And if you go to an AA meeting on Monday night, they know that, too."

"And . . . ?"

"Those women are terrified of you," he said. "They don't run from a woman who's drunk at the country club on Saturday night. But when you're the only woman in town who's got the courage to go to AA meetings, they don't want to *talk* to you and they don't want to *know* you because they don't want to look at the idea that it's OK to be a reformed drunk."

When I visited there two years later, a waitress at the restaurant walked up to me and said, "I just want to tell you, lady, that because you went to AA meetings, I'm going now, too." And that was enough for me—right there. Nothing else mattered.


After I'd been sober a few years, I searched and searched to find some purpose in life—where I was accomplishing something and being fulfilled by it. "Please, God, help me find a purpose," I used to pray. When I got to AA, my main purpose seemed to be in pleasing others so they would think I was OK, and that would make me feel OK in the process. Working in order to make money also wasn't fun anymore. *What am I here for? What am I about?* I didn't come here to get rich and buy clothes. All those things are nice, but that's not my purpose either.

I read a tiny book that suggested writing down fifteen personality aspects about yourself that you like. Then picking several that you want to be centered in—those you feel strongest about. In putting that together, I saw my purpose in life.

Young women come into the AA fellowship not knowing that they are empowered, and I want to help them find it. And, of course, the more I help them, the more I'll find my own. By "empowerment," I mean allowing Spirit to express within me. Most of us have squelched that.

A significant shift occurred for me when I was eight years' sober. I moved to Sedona, Arizona, and didn't have a sponsor. The only two women in the fellowship there didn't have what I wanted, so I was kind of lost. It may have been foolish on my part, but I couldn't find a woman to work with. However, one of the men had been sober eighteen years. He was a bachelor about my age, and I wasn't attracted to him, but I liked his program. I liked what he was about. I liked what he talked about. And I saw him making decisions in his own life that were working. So one night when I was really crazy, I walked up to him and said, "Rick, would you be my sponsor?"

"Well, God knows you need one!" he said with a grin, as he amiably shook his head.

We went for coffee, and he told me, "Sarah Beth, I'm sure that you've written many inventories, but I want you to write an inventory about God . . . I want to know your relationship with God."

At that point I was still thinking that when I found the answer to life and lived it well, then I was going to be OK.

I wrote three paragraphs and realized that my relationship with God was exactly the same as it was with my mother: "I won't do any more bad things, and I'll strive to be a good girl. I promise to get a gold star by learning my lessons perfectly. And if I do it just right, you'll make a space for me, and you'll love me."

That exercise stripped away all my old concepts and made me realize that a true "God" would not work that way—*He loved me no matter what!* I don't have to prove anything; I don't have to be good; I don't have to be anything other than Sarah Beth. That's all God wants from me.

I gained my freedom and learned the true meaning of forgiveness—that *I* was forgiven. I couldn't be enough to please Mother, but I was OK with God.

And I never did reach the point where I pleased Mother. I'm sorry to say it, but it's been easier since she's been gone. Our relationship improved when my relationship with myself and my God got better, but she was still after me the last week of her life: "I hate you," she growled. "I've always hated you, and I don't see any way it's ever gonna be different."

"Mother, you don't have to live with such venom," I told her. "I know how you feel. But you don't have to do that to yourself anymore."

I know it's a strange thing for a mother to say, but she was an angry, unhappy woman. She didn't drink, but she exhibited all the destructive behavior, especially the spontaneous rage, of a chronic alcoholic.


When I realized that God's love for me was unlimited and unconditional, I came to believe in the empowerment of Spirit. I believe that when God gave me breath, He breathed His life into me and gave me power and freedom. I didn't sense that growing up, and I decided that getting drunk would free me enough to feel powerful.

For a long time, I thought God was separate from me, and as long as I felt that way, I felt empty and unloved. Now I teach a woman that she has Spirit inside that empowers her.

I'm grateful to know the love I know today, the powerful presence I feel within me. When I forget (and today was a hectic Monday when the world wasn't very good), I have to remember to take a deep breath and recall that Spirit is always present within me, and it's quite enough.

And then I'm at peace.

Along the way, I've needed to put my expectations in perspective, because they weren't realistic—searching for the right man and the correct circumstances so I could be happy. And, of course, none of that worked. I had to get rid of those old ideas.

As a successful independent businesswoman and drinking buddy, I'd always known how to be one of the guys. I still do. But today I have very good women friends who . . . oh, I just love them so dearly. We are totally open with each other and talk about every-thing. They're such a wonderful part of my life.

And I find that permeating other areas. This week I went to a medical office where the receptionist, the nurse practitioner, and the doctor are all female. I found myself surrounded by these well-prepared women, who are so loving and supportive—a tight-knit group all helping each other. As I walked out, I thought, *Gosh, I feel like I've been to a meeting.*

Today I have a comfort zone that allows me to be with women without feeling separate or ashamed of myself in any way. I don't have to compare anymore. Before, I wouldn't be around other women. Sometimes I felt betrayed by them; at other times, belit-tled. And I definitely never felt I was enough. Some of those feelings legitimately arose from criticism, but most originated in my mind. Now I feel totally supported by women in all areas of my life, whether at church, socially, or in the business world. And I know it's because of the way *I* look at life.

"It's not what you're looking *at* that you see," I once read. "It's what you're looking *with*."[1]

People today often comment on my gentleness. Even in a department store, a sales clerk will remark, "You have the most compassionate look in your eyes." I've had several strange women come up to me and say, "I'm sorry to bother you, ma'am, but I want to tell you that you have the kindest way about you." It must be the way I'm looking at them because in my heart I feel a deep love and respect for people. And I never had that until I experi-enced the kind of love I found in AA. That's the Higher Power, the power I always looked for, the God in my life that I dreamed of, the man in my world that I always wanted—and now I have it with everybody.

Virtually every young woman I get to know, whether as a sponsor or friend, feels the same way I once did: being a woman, they feel "less than." They may cover it up by appearing sexy or by acting aggressive in the business world, but inside there's that hole that says, "You just aren't enough. You don't quite measure up."

Even now, the world is geared more toward men. Whether in religion, in business, or in society, women have been overprotected or set aside as too fragile. They may be good concepts put there for our protection, or they may be put there for control, but what happens is that we get the idea that we're just not quite enough to make it.

What I found in myself and in young women coming into the program—very capable, independent businesswomen—is that we felt "less than" until we found a Higher Power that empowered us.

How do we start? By recognizing that the whole world isn't about us, although we have a hard time with that because our lives have been about what "I'm doing," and how "I feel," and what "I want." And that's not the way the world works—it's certainly not the way God works. We're not going to be empowered until we move away from the center of life. If we stay there, we'll never be satisfied because being self-centered and needy are sides of the same coin.

Then we need the possibility of forgiveness in our lives. And once a woman sees that she can forgive and be forgiven, fear will no longer rule her. Practicing forgiveness, as well as tolerance and open-mindedness, will dissipate her fears.

At the same time, a young woman needs to establish healthy boundaries. Until I learned to say "No," I needed your approval. At first, I couldn't say "No" to you. Grew up that way. Never had any boundaries—didn't know what they were. "Say 'yes' when you mean 'yes,' and 'no' when you mean 'no,' " the Bible says, just as clear as can be. Seems too simple to be real. But until I learned to say "No" to you, I had no power.

Once I got sober, I thought everything would be beautiful, no problems, and I would know what to do all the time. But that's not true.

I had to learn that the last step says "practice, practice, practice." And if I want to practice setting appropriate boundaries, then I have to learn how to say "Yes" when I mean yes and "No" when I mean no. Otherwise, I'll be pleasing you and hurting me. When we're doing it, we don't think it's a lie to say "Yes" when we mean "No," but it is. Suddenly, I've just given myself away. So I really have to practice more and more on truth. I do.

My grandma once saw me off on a plane going across the world and said, "Honey, I was born fifty years too soon." Then when she turned ninety, she told us, "I've never been on an airplane and I never swam in the ocean—and I'm doing both before I die." She chartered a plane, took her girlfriends (the youngest of whom was eighty-seven) to the coast, and swam in the Atlantic. I've got precious pictures of them on the beach, with their dresses ballooning up from the ocean breeze. That's the kind of spirit I always want to have—and it's accessible, inside of me.

# 21

## DON'T GET STRESSED OUT IN THE DARK
## LISTENING TO SLOW MUSIC

◼

For every alcoholic who can point to a parent with the same disorder, there are several others who have no such heritage. How did they get it? The answer has to be in environmental causes.

Back we go to the study of animals.

When left alone, animals uniformly prefer a natural beverage. In other words, strains of alcohol-preferring mice have to be specially bred. Cats, too. Never having been seduced by the allure of the Bud Girls or the captain of the football team, cats ordinarily have no reason to overcome their natural abhorrence to the taste of alcohol—unless they are subjected to repeated stress, that is. Then they prefer to drink an alcoholic "milk cocktail" instead of plain milk.[1]

Experiments with ordinary water-preferring rats also demonstrate that when they're placed under severe stress, induced by random electrical shocks, they, too, develop a preference for alcohol. And they continue to belly up to the bar—and even increase their intake—long after the experimental shocks are stopped.[2]

Most interestingly, rats also develop a strong preference for alcohol while living in total darkness. And they only partially change these nocturnal habits when forced to live in constant light. In fact, putting them back into normal lighting conditions results in a relapse to drinking levels reached during total darkness.[3]

Meanwhile, studies of nightclub patrons have shown that the slower the music, the faster the customers consume alcohol.[4]

Momma was right—never marry an entertainer, bartender, or waitress who sleeps days and works nights in a country western bar.

Not surprisingly, women in relationships with heavy drinkers often do become addicted themselves. But for most of us, both stress at work and the bar scene are temporary conditions with passing influence.

What affects us most is the culture in which we live. . . .

# 22

## GOD CREATED ALCOHOL SO THE IRISH WOULDN'T CONQUER THE WORLD
### —and the Chinese Would

◨

For many men and women, heavy social drinking over several years, the equivalent of three to five beers a day, is a part of the normal addictive process.[1] But most people don't start there. They gradually work up to it. And if they do, they're greatly influenced by one thing—the culture in which they live.

Irish men raise pint after pint with a group of their mates at the pub because that is integral to their culture. As a result, they develop addiction seven times more often than men of Mediterranean descent.[2]

Jewish men don't drink much because that's not part of what it means to be Jewish. The French, meanwhile, are among the world leaders in addiction because heavy wine consumption is synonymous with being French. And the Asian people, whose societies for generations seemed naturally devoid of alcohol addiction, find their problems rising with increased contact with Western cultural norms.

### Why Bars Are Not Guarded

Momentous drinking shifts do occur.

In Islam, abstinence spread rapidly among the religion's early converts when a fortress fell in their heavy drinking culture because of a drunk night guard.[3]

In Turkey, drinking behavior went the opposite direction. Parliament long debated whether beer was an alcoholic drink and therefore subject to the powerful cultural and legal restrictions on drinking. Finally, laws were passed permitting the sale of beer in traditional coffeehouses and *kebab* restaurants, both of which were soon converted into pubs. TV commercials promoting beer saturated the airwaves, and it soon replaced coffee and sweets as the traditional offering to guests in the Turkish home.[4]

Native-American tribes for centuries contained the use of mind-altering substances through their sacred cultural traditions. However, a new substance—alcohol—was introduced into their midst at the same time their culture was being forcibly obliterated. As a result, few tribes were able to build the necessary social and religious sanctions circumscribing alcohol's use. The tribes that were able to do so are practically abstinent, but most were unable to react quickly enough and were decimated by rampant drinking.[5]

A similar effect has been observed among Australian aborigines and Eskimos.[6]

## If Only I Could Remember It the Next Day

Although the normal drinking pattern in society as a whole strongly influences our conduct,[7] the key determinant is the behavior of friends and colleagues—the culture surrounding our work and social life.

Writers, lawyers, musicians, brokers, salespeople, and company executives, for instance, have historically lived the romanticized "work hard/play hard" lifestyle. Myth has it that the best scripts, lyrics, trial strategies, and marketing ideas were often conjured in a bar. How could anyone excel without being a legendary drinker like the great ghosts of old? After all, according to their biographers, four of the first seven Americans to win the Nobel Prize for literature were alcoholics, and another—John Steinbeck—drank heavily.[8]

In many professions, freedom from supervision appears to be an important contributing factor to heavy alcohol use. When there's no boss to notice and respond to excessive drinking, a person is free to indulge at will.

## We Like to Drink, Ltd.

Not only are people influenced by the established culture in their profession, but they will often create their own culture.

Heavy drinkers frequently find each other for relationships, business and personal, unconsciously seeking comfort in a false sense of normalcy. In effect, they fashion their own personal and occupational subculture.

Women, as an example, tend to drink like their partners, best friends, or coworkers—birds of a feather get snockered together—with voluntary selection certainly playing a role here: "I think I'll land in the beer pond, thank you." On the other hand, a woman who has a drinking problem and is close to several nondrinkers would make the endangered species list.[9]

Construction workers in England and Wales at one time formed a drinking group that beat out even brewery employees in consumption, with 18 percent averaging more than fifty drinks a week. No big shock that construction company executives, according to urine lab tests, minimized their drinking more than the manual laborers.[10] When it comes to alcohol, *sophistication kills.*

The heavier the drinking, the more it occurs in bars. Why? Probably because that is the culture left when a person gradually and unknowingly dissociates from normal friends. Even there, the subculture of the group has its impact: tavern drinkers in Canada, the U.S., and the Netherlands, for example, each were found to consume more as part of a group than when drinking alone.[11] "Come on . . . have another one."

## Moving to a Land of Beer and Money

The powerful impact of culture can best be seen when people emigrate. In Mexico, there is strong disapproval of drinking by women. When they move to the U.S.A., those who readily accept the new American way of life are *nine* times more likely to be heavy drinkers than women who cling to their old culture.[12]

## I'm in Love, Pass the Rice Wine

With today's global economy and world media, it is not necessary to move anywhere to be affected by another culture. This is best seen in Asia, where alcohol was not a problem for centuries.

Scientists thought for years that many Asians were naturally immune to developing an addiction to alcohol. Here's why. The liver ordinarily produces enough of two enzymes to break down alcohol; the first converts it into acetaldehyde, a poison, and the second neutralizes this toxin. But Asians of Mongoloid origin—which includes about one-third to one-half of all Japanese, Koreans, and Chinese—happen to have a genetic deficiency of the second enzyme. As a result, moderate drinking leaves poisonous acetaldehyde in their systems, which causes facial flushing, increased heart rate, a hot sensation in the stomach, and heart palpitations—none of which are conducive to more drinking.

Researchers naturally assumed, then, that this genetic protection was a *barrier* against addiction. But many native North Americans are also of Mongoloid origin, having originally migrated from Asia, and have similar enzyme deficiencies. That fact and the escalating rate of addiction in Asia are making it abundantly clear that this genetic anomaly is not a barrier but only a hurdle that can easily be overcome.

With hindsight, what appeared to be *genetic* protection was in reality a *cultural* safeguard constructed of ancient principles that limited drinking to special circumstances. That shield is crumbling, however, with the growing adoption of modern Western norms.

The drinking customs of Japanese men, for instance, have evolved so rapidly that they may have already surpassed their Western counterparts. Studies comparing the drinking habits and problems of Japanese men, U.S. Caucasians, and Japanese Americans conclude that men in Japan drink much more frequently—62 percent partaking at least three times a week.[13] According to a separate national survey, 37 percent of Japanese men drink every day.[14] Much of the feasting occurs around social and business activities that have become part of the cultural fabric. Not surprisingly, Japanese men also admit to drinking greater amounts than American men and having the most alcohol-related problems. One in four report blackouts, feeling the effects of drinking while at work, being advised to cut back, and feeling the need to slow down.[15]

No doubt the austere work ethic in Japan creates significant stress, which can be temporarily relieved with alcohol, now that cultural restrictions have eased.

Remarkable change has also swept over Korea, where 500 years of Confucian structure and self-discipline has given way to a society of men known as the "Irish of Asia." Men socialize in groups, drinking heavily, keeping up with their colleagues and friends.[16] They take turns buying rounds of drinks, sometimes insisting that their fellows drink to their maximum ability. Drunkenness is not only tolerated but actually encouraged, with latecomers proudly consuming three rapid drinks to catch up. As a result, an astounding 42 percent of Korean men exhibit symptoms of alcohol abuse or dependence at some point in their lives.[17]

At the moment, there's still little drinking and drunkenness in China's culture, but it is growing in the Chinese business class, driven by affluence and exposure to Western standards.

# 23

## KEVIN

■

You know that you've got a problem, but you hear of guys who've been in jail, who are living in a rehab or halfway house or what-have-you. And your first reaction is, "Jesus, I've still got a house in Fiji and a house in Australia, and I've got a sailing yacht and three cars and two factories going—and it's still alive. It's not *healthy,* but it's going. And I'm not nearly in jail."

So I'm not in that class. But it wouldn't have taken too much longer. It *would* have happened.

It had been suggested in the family and by a good friend of my wife's that I ought to go and get help. At that stage, I thought *they* needed help! It had got to a point where business wasn't doing well and was going crooked. I was blaming her end of the involvement in the business, the government's policies—just about everybody I could think of. It surely wasn't *me.* Because when things went askew, I'd go and have a couple of drinks and solve the world's problems on a drink coaster. I'd write out my new business plan on that. But nothing new would happen. No changes.

I was running a business that was offshore and interstate— probably a bit of escapism in that you're always going somewhere. And traveling regularly is an easy way to hide. On the airplanes you can get as much booze as you want, if you want. And there's nothing unusual about getting off a plane half full. And hotel room fridges are full all the time, aren't they? Plus different people all the time. Somebody in business who travels a bit can hide it much better than someone who's stuck in one spot.

When you're full-blown drinking, getting on an airplane is a lot of fun. I used to be scared of the things unless I was half full. They don't worry me at all now. The Serenity prayer takes the planes up in the air.

When I was blowin' and goin', I would insist on having things my way. I'd say, "We gotta do this"—so we'd go and do it. In the process, we built a business in five states of Australia, across the water in New Zealand, and across the water in Fiji. And quite complicated—with manufacturing, wholesaling, and retailing.

So I had become fairly godlike as far as knowledge was concerned and couldn't be told much. I'm *still* not real good at being told stuff, but I'm getting better at it!

I'm not sure where the trolley fell off. I tend to think some of it was me not owning up to things that were happening, which I couldn't solve—and that had to be changed. Because the world in almost any industry has not only gotten smaller, it's also changing bloody quickly now.

Occasionally, I'd have the feeling, *I've got to stop drinking.* But then I'd think, *I'll get off the grog when I solve the day's problems.* Obviously the problems got bigger as my intake got bigger. So it wasn't going away.

I got to the stage in life where you'd say, "Stop the world, I want to get off." I'd had enough of it, and not necessarily for the right reasons.

I didn't have a drinking problem, I figured, because I didn't start in the mornings. But then I eventually started at ten, so that's early enough, isn't it? At the end, it became a one-hour episode in between. Every hour I'd have to go for a walk and have a big double vodka. And I needed it, you know, to take everything away. But as far as me having a problem, I don't know what actually made me think I had the problem because I figured the *family* had the problem, the *business* had the problem, and I was the one trying to sort all the problems out. And I needed the drink because I was doing such a good job keeping everything together. Not only needed it—*deserved* it!

Early one morning, after one of the holiday parties that wasn't going to be a party, I knew I couldn't do it anymore. Oh, it was just chaotic! I'd come in with a couple of blokes—I don't even know who they were—out of a pub in Red Sand, which is pretty bottom-end of the world over here. And I brought them home and promptly got kicked out. Then I woke up in the morning and really knew I'd hit the pits. Because they'd robbed me, too, these guys. I didn't even have my keys or any money left. Nothing!

And it had been coming, too. I'd been waking up in the morning and thinking, *Oh, God, another bloody day.* And it would be no better than the day before.

By Christmas Day, I'd finally had enough. Christmas in our family had been a disaster for the last ten years. Having a factory, we'd always have a party, which would be a drunken ball and orgy and what-have-you. And one day after, sometimes not knowing what the hell had happened.

At the last one, I'd ended up still at the factory the following morning with a carton of beer and no friends. Not like in the old days, when we'd have a bunch still going. At least I'd have had two or three people with me. It had got to that stage where you finished up on your own—still going.

The time had come round where the family pushing didn't matter anymore because it wasn't the family. Finally, it was *me.* I had decided I'd had enough. The family could have pushed me for the next twenty years and it wouldn't have made a difference. I had to fight with the problem.


I went to a local meeting where some reasonably good guys went, and if there's such a thing as an upmarket meeting, this was an upmarket meeting. A couple of doctors go there, and some of them are still doing quite well—or have put themselves back into that position. Whereas a couple of other meetings that I now attend, if I'd have thought of going there first, I'd have never gone back because I just wouldn't have identified at all.

Like everybody else, I couldn't imagine doing anything without having a grog. I couldn't imagine going to a function, a luncheon, or anything else without having one. I suppose like every other alcoholic, I thought, *What the hell do you do if you don't drink?* I didn't know. Well, I do many things now, and it doesn't really worry me.

By six months of sobriety, I had worked out a business plan to have everything resurrected, smartened out, and straightened up. And everything would be back in good shape. I felt pretty good— but nothing happened. The numbers didn't get better.

End of the second year, if anything, it was probably marginally worse. Well, I say marginally worse, but possibly not marginally worse; possibly I was just more honest with the figures. A frightening thought dawned on me: *Unless things change and change dramatically, you've got to get out.*

I had gone through the middle part of that second year where I wanted to get out of the business entirely, and I'd have been happy doing nothing and getting a bedroll. But then I got into that third year and realized, "You're still gonna have to work, gonna have to do something. And there's no reason that you can't still be successful. It can be much better than it ever was if we can just get our act together again—but properly this time."

And by now, into the start of the fourth year, we've had some pretty heavy changes that have taken the pressure out of it. Haven't put much fun back in it yet—I've sold a few possessions, big ones—but we're going to make it.

For many of us, we're the big guy with a business, living in the best house in Fiji and one of the better ones on the harbor in Sydney, and on the surface that looks terrific to everybody. But you've got huge payments—and you don't own the bank—and every morning you're worried about paying everybody.

That's gone now. We've come to a reasonable, much more modest lifestyle. The aim is to owe very little money and not be so position hungry. That way, we can have a bit of peace, instead of going to work worrying, "If we don't make ten grand today, I'm in trouble tomorrow." That sort of pressure could lead back to drinking.


A few changes do come about in sobriety. You are not chasing the same sort of things; now you're simply chasing a bit more freedom, a bit more time. I've always had a yacht, and the last five years, while I was still drinking, I didn't sail it often. I'd go down there and act as if I were working on it, but I'd have a carton of drinks with me.

Now I rarely fail, whichever country I'm in—Australia or Fiji—to go sailing every week. I'm having good fun getting back into that and making some buddies. I'm considering heading for—if not this year, then next—the World Championships for the Masters, which are the forty-five to fifty-four age group. And after that, they've got the fifty-four to sixty, which is the Grand Masters. And I've started good.

But, you know, I wouldn't have done that while I was still drinking. It's the last sort of event I would have gone in for. We did very well in others, but they were events where you could buy the sailors and the gear. If you have the right people and the best equipment, you know you'll win.

To go into a single-handed class, where everybody gets a boat that's exactly the same, you've got to be good. There's nothing you can do to make yourself better—unless you *are* better. I'm taking third, fourth, or fifth now, but I'm trying hard. The difference, I suppose, is the ego is not the same. I go out and enjoy it. If I'm not enjoying it, I'll turn it in and say, "Oh, bugger this." Now I'm doing things more for pleasure than for show.

What's terrific in the Fijis is that at least one AA cruising yacht pulls in each summer and winter season, and with me being a sailor, I've accompanied them down through the island groups. In New Zealand, I landed at a meeting and mentioned sailing a bit, and the next day, I got a phone call at the hotel. And what do we do? We go sailing on a yacht. Just a couple of the boys, say. And that doesn't happen in the old system—not my old system, anyway.

I haven't yelled at the Fijians for, oh, maybe two years now. In the islands, you can tell somebody how to do something, and while you're watching for the next five minutes, they'll do it that way. And then you walk away and come back with half an hour gone, and they're back to the old system. You can be pissed all the time. Other people would throw hammers around the building and swear and call an employee names and get nowhere. For me, it comes back to the thought process I've learned in the program—thinking before acting, and then acting reasonably.

Probably the last four or five years of drinking, the thinking in between going for the next grog was how to get over the problem directly in front of me. And everything else I wasn't worried about. As far as thinking about other people and how they'd react, or whether it would give me a problem next week, I'd do anything just to get out of a problem that day.

Whereas now, I can think a bit further ahead and say, "Look, that's a good short-term solution, but what'll happen six months down the track? Jesus, that's gonna build a long-term problem. So let's not do it."

Before, I'd have read maybe five books in ten years. And that would have been only at the rare times we went on holiday. Now, almost a book a week. Not highly intelligent stuff, but the best-selling novels.

Probably for twenty years, there was drink and money. Then positions. And that was it. Then the wheels fell out from under, and, mind you, it didn't matter for a while there because I didn't think I had long to go anyway. And now I think if I could give up my smokes, I've probably got thirty or forty years to go.

I don't really think I have to plan years ahead. But three of the guys at the meeting I went to last night aren't working, and they're living in sort of shed houses and get their 160 bucks a week, or whatever, from the government. And in another year they'll decide to go look for a job. They're living one day at a time, one hour at a time. There's nothing wrong with that—and it's appealing at times. But if you're still in a business and running it, you've got things that you must do to make it to the end of the year. So it's very hard to just be day-to-day.

On the other hand, I heard somebody say the other day that the prayer says, "Give us this day our daily bread." And the guy said, "You know, I really want my monthly bread, and I want my annual bread, and I want my ten-year bread, but God just seems to give me daily bread." So maybe we don't have to worry about the next thirty years.


As far as the drink's concerned, I no longer think about it very often. I haven't had to ring up a buddy for probably six months now. It used to be, "Aw, Jesus, things are terrible, and I might as well go and have a grog." I haven't felt that in a long time.

I still go to meetings because if I didn't mix with them I don't think I'd last—particularly in the islands. Most of the expatriates over there drink. Or put it this way: around the sailing club they all drink, and all the business guys drink. A hell of a lot. There's nobody over there to even *talk* to.

And in Fiji, the people in recovery have more fun. We're all good friends. I also enjoy going to meetings in Australia and try to do three a week. I just don't know too many people who have stopped going—that tells you something. If it becomes a drudge, I might. Hell no, I don't think so.

It's a bit of pressure at home from time to time, and they say, "Well, Jesus, we don't see you any more than we used to."

In the early stages, when that comment would be made, I'd say, "Look, I'll go and get a bottle of wine instead." But I don't bother with that anymore.

There's still the occasional, "How long are you going to keep doing this?"

And I say, "Well, Dr. John's over twenty-five years and still going."

It's hard to get people to understand the remarkable camaraderie and friendship and fellowship that adds so much to life.

Sydney was an easy place to be an alcoholic businessman because it's such a big city and you get lost in it. When I was working here all the time, I could go to a different pub every day, whereas you get over in the Fijis and you become more prominent because there are only three or four places. And it's not long before you spot the businessmen parked with a couple of brown paper bags in their hand.

Talking to them is much harder than talking to somebody who's really hit rock bottom. When I say rock bottom, some of these guys have gone as low as you want to go. But maybe they just haven't fallen far enough to ask for help.

Successful men and women are fairly hard to convince unless they've hit the wall and gone bust. All I can tell you is that you will hit the wall if you stay at it. Accomplished people are a difficult breed. Mainly because they know it all anyway, don't they? Or think they do.

In international business, it's easy to do a geographical. A guy gets chopped out of Fiji after two years and goes to Thailand, where he'll last probably another two years. But to even suggest he has a problem is like—well, you couldn't.

And people sometimes are unwittingly supportive of practicing alcoholics. One bloke had a problem for a long time, but he hasn't got it at the moment. He had it when his wife first decided to leave him, and he had it up until he got a girlfriend. Now, it's gone away. I've had a good yam with him, and I thought that he was worse than me, to be honest, but, yeah, you can hide it, particularly with the support of other people.

Trouble is, although you can hide from others, you can't run from yourself.

But even when you face the personal cost inflicted by drinking, the most difficult admission is that your business life is unmanageable. For example, we used to manufacture in Singapore. In being honest, I realized that Singapore was more an ego trip than about making dollars. I'd gotten the business out of control, and it was necessary to bring it back to being manageable. It either had to be much bigger and employ better people, or get smaller, where we were competent enough to handle it—which I'll admit now, but never could before.

And there's a fair bit of pain in doing that and in admitting that, although we were doing some things in Fiji very well, others weren't being done well enough. And in admitting that we should change direction and manufacture some of our product elsewhere, after spending so much time defending the place that I'd almost brainwashed everybody into believing that was the only way you could go.

And I'm convinced we still have to change directions. We're better off going without the volume and concentrating on a certain section and doing that very, very well. It makes no sense to produce four times as many versions and make them three-quarters as well because you don't stay alive anymore unless your merchandise is bloody good.

We own the company. If we didn't, I'd probably have left two years ago. Now I'm starting to feel better. It's got every chance of doing very well again, but I'm not trying to do everything all the time now either. In fact, I'm possibly doing less than other people, but doing it better. I wasn't a real flash at delegating before, but I'm getting better.

I'm not perfect at running the business yet; I just look at it through different eyes. Like paying accounts on time. Before, I'd do anything not to pay them if there was a way to get out of 'em. I suppose that's all in coming back to being quite more honest now.

I'm starting to get myself cleaned up with the taxation department as well, which is good. And I'm cleaning some hidden areas that used to worry the hell out of me. That was accomplished by owning up to a few things that were bothering me. I no longer worry, "Is he gonna find that out and drop a brick on me one day?" Now it's all aboveboard. And the government can come in, have a look, and I'm just not gonna panic anymore, whereas the mere mention of them on the phone used to send me running.

There's still a bit to go, and mainly it's still centered around the family, where I've been called more selfish now than I used to be. I'm not sure whether that's in fact correct, or whether it's that I stand up for myself now. Before I was in the wrong so much of the time that I'd give in, even when I was right. Now I can get a bit too righteous.

My son used to be in the business with me, in addition to my wife and daughter. But if anything went wrong, I had a bad habit of screaming at anybody in our family and going easy on people we employed. My son may come back one day—we're friends again. That's taken two-and-a-half years.

But probably the single best feeling is I don't feel guilty about anything I've done in the last year. I can wake up knowing that I haven't wronged the family. I might have been cross, but I haven't done anything desperate or dishonest, and nobody's going to ring up tomorrow and say, "I saw him last with so-and-so in a bar at such-and-such." I'm just not worried about it anymore. And that type of fear, that sort of guilt, hurts a lot.

I never thought it hurt me until I didn't have it anymore. Now I consciously know that my wife can ring me if I'm in Fiji by myself, and I can tell her every single thing that happened because there's nothing to hide. Whereas before, it would be a series of half-truths. And yet, I've still got some work on the homefront to get everything as comfortable as it should be. But that's probably just working on things that I should've been working on for thirty years and never did.

About communicating feelings: never been very good at that and still not. I'd go to some meetings where everybody gives you a hug, and I would freeze. I'm sort of losing that now, but that's just something with me.

When I was drinking, if I had to talk to the staff as a group or give a small speech at some function, I'd have to drink three doubles ahead of time. And then I'd still be nervous. For some reason, now it's gone the other way 'round. Yeah, I'm quite comfortable in front of a group and in meeting new people. That doesn't just come out of not drinking. It's something I learned by going to meetings. They help my confidence and get me feeling more relaxed. I mean, if I don't know something—hell, I don't know it. Whereas before, I knew everything.

I've been in this industry for twenty years, and I've probably learned more in the last nine months than I've ever learned, simply because my mind's open again.

When I used to travel, I'd meet somebody in a bar and never talk to them again. But now I make terrific friends wherever I go. Ten guys I can ring up and talk to, you know, because I actually come away with names and numbers from other countries. Whereas before, I wouldn't want to remember who I'd been with.

It's a different world and a helluva lot better. And I'm mindful now when I'm speaking with someone who's got a problem . . . How do you explain? There's just a bit more thought process goes into everything, I s'pose, isn't there?

# 24

## NICOLE

◪

My husband was a military man and they stationed us in Germany. When I had a baby there, at age twenty-two, I had difficulty nursing, so several German women advised me, "If you want to nurse, drink some beer. It helps the milk flow."

"You must be kidding!" I said.

But at that time, some Germans actually did put beer in their babies' bottles, and new mothers who couldn't relax enough to nurse were told to drink beer. I refused because I didn't want to be like my mother. So we ended up putting Harry on a bottle because it wasn't working the other way.

By the time my baby was a year old, I had become very lonely being in another country and had started suffering from insomnia. One night we went to a party attended by my doctor, and he joked, "I know how you can get to sleep: I'm prescribing that you get drunk every night!"

When I saw him at the office, he said, "I'm serious. I think you should drink at least two of those big, strong German beers a night."

"OK," I said, and discovered it to be a good cure. But that was the beginning of the end.

The Germans, you see, as well as members of the American community over there, drank large quantities of beer, and it was socially accepted. Before I started drinking, people would ask me if I was a Mormon because I didn't drink, smoke, or use coffee.

But I soon became one of those happy party women. I loved to dance and I didn't care with whom. If my husband didn't want to dance, I'd go after anybody in the whole place who would, even Germans with whom I couldn't communicate—it just didn't matter. My husband and our friends would say, "Well, where is she? She's gone." And they'd have to go find me.

We lived in Munich, and Oktoberfest was fantastic. Thousands of people in this huge tent, just drinking and drinking. We loved it. Friends would come from all over Germany to stay with us, and we'd take them because we knew the ropes. But they always had to make sure where I was. Otherwise, they'd have no idea if I was still there. I didn't wander off many times, but enough to frighten me.

The first time I ever got real drunk was in the winter at a recipe-book promotion, after I'd had a second boy. We were all young women in our twenties, trying all kinds of drinks. Well, on the way home to our old German house, I dropped my baby in the snow. I was told later what had happened because I didn't remember any of it. And it scared me to death.

After that I hardly ever drank in public. At home, I never cared for the beer the doctor prescribed, but I liked rum and Coke. So I'd wait till my boys and my husband were asleep, fill our pond-size bathtub with hot water, make these great big drinks, and soak and read and drink. . . .

Eventually, we were transferred to Hawaii, where I sold dictation equipment to attorneys, doctors, and institutions. I was on the road and could do pretty much what I wanted. We lived on one side of the island, and I worked and drank on the other. I would start drinking after work with friends in a tropical park, drive home over the mountain, and wake up the next morning thinking, *How did I get here?* No one else ever knew; I never even received a traffic ticket.

All during this time I was training for the Hawaiian Marathon, so I would run every day, sometimes doing ten miles, and then up to twenty when I was ready. In between, we'd race a 10K some-where almost every weekend, and then we'd all hang around and drink beer. My husband and my boys were running, too, and that saved my marriage for a long time.

I trained for the marathon every morning and then got drunk

every night. It's amazing what you can do. I would meet one of my running partners, and then in the middle of our run up on Diamond Head, I would have to stop every once in a while, bend over, and throw up.

I also belonged to a running club in Hawaii. We would run all over the island and then we'd gather and drink ourselves silly. People would moon and do crazy things. It was fun for a while, but finally I quit going because I couldn't trust myself. I'd go to the parties and be polite, and then go home and finish drinking. But every few months I just needed to get out and really party with people, and then some humiliating event would happen.

I was in beautiful Waikiki, unhappy in my marriage, and all these gorgeous tourists were around. At times I'd get drunk, pick one up, and wake up in some hotel room. Most embarrassing, I went to my girlfriend's house with the kids once, left with her twenty-year-old neighbor, and came back with hickeys all over my neck.

I finally went to my husband and said, "There's something wrong here. This is not OK, and I need help." He reacted by going out and getting drunk and not coming home for two days.

In reality, all I wanted was to get out of the marriage, but I didn't know how. He kept saying no, and for some reason, rather than leave, I kept acting out.

I'm convinced now that with the right tools and good counseling that marriage could have been saved.


After we got divorced, I stayed depressed and kept having one crisis after another. Eventually, I went for some counseling with the preacher, and he asked me, "Do you think how much you drink has anything to do with this depression and chaos in your life?"

It was like a lightning bolt exploded in my head: "Somebody knows besides me!" It was quite a relief. He suggested that I call some of my friends at the church and join them for an AA meeting. Apparently, several of the people I hung out with went to meetings and knew about me, but I had no clue.

Scared and shaky, I went to a noon meeting at the YMCA in downtown Honolulu; and I was so impressed that famous people were there. Many tourists attend that meeting, and they always ask for visitors in the beginning. My friend who took me said, "You can just sit there. You don't have to say anything." I *couldn't* have talked. I just cried, went home, and got drunk.

I wasn't ready.

For months at the end of the meeting, when they said the Lord's Prayer, I would cry—because I knew I was home but still had this inner struggle going on and couldn't stop drinking completely.

My home group consisted of men. It was small and intimate and they would joke with me, "Well, you're not an alcoholic because (a) you're a woman, (b) you don't smoke, and (c) you won't drink coffee!" But they were real supportive, and they all agreed to be my surrogate sponsors until I could get a female sponsor. But they insisted that I go to meetings all over the island.

I went to meetings three months before I stayed sober, and those were some of the most painful days in my life. I'd admitted to the whole world that there was really a problem, and that I had found the solution, but for some reason I just couldn't do it.

In that period, people would say to me, "Just surrender."

"How?" I'd ask.

They told me that I was still trying to run the show. More than one person told me the same thing, using different words, but when I didn't hear what I wanted to hear, I'd call somebody else. Finally, I realized that to "surrender" means to give up on my old idea that somehow I could drink, and to give up on how it was working before, because it didn't.

To "surrender," "let go," "throw in the towel," or "drop the rock" means to be willing to listen. Be willing to get still and hear what the truth is.

To this day I don't know how to tell somebody to surrender, but I know how to do it. I have to be alone and stop the chatter—be quiet and listen, or drive and listen, or clean house and listen. During the first months of my sobriety, there was so much chatter in my head, I constantly kept this track going with the Serenity prayer*—over and over.

"Surrendering" means to surrender to how it is. I had a friend I'd call, whining and moaning and complaining about my life. He would say, "What's the key?"

---

*"God, grant me the serenity to accept the things I cannot change. Courage to change the things I can. And the wisdom to know the difference."

I would sigh and complete the mantra: "Acceptance." In other words, accepting life on life's terms, being OK with it the way it is, not trying to fight and struggle all the time.

As a saleswoman, I was different things to various people. There was no person who knew every facet of Nicole—including Nicole. So I had to seek professional help, just to look at all of it, and be willing to tell the truth, the whole truth, to one person—and to get a sponsor who would get to know and understand me.

It's been twelve years, and I honestly don't think I'll ever drink again. I go to my meetings. I call my sponsor, work the twelve steps, do my prayer and meditation. That works. And I found out the hard way—that's the way it works for me.

As part of my program, I have a morning routine. When I first wake up, I listen to a meditation tape. Then I read some thoughts for the day, followed by a positive affirmation from a prosperity book—because I want more abundance in my life. Last, I read a little book named *God Calling.* Over the years, I've gradually added more. From talking with people who have over ten years of sobriety, I decided that it takes more to stay enchanted than before.

When I first got sober, just to read one thought for the day or one page in the Big Book was a major accomplishment. Over time, I've disciplined myself because I've learned that I tend to be an undisciplined person, and that self-discipline gives me the freedom I want. If I don't, my life becomes chaotic.

Today I'm a single mom with a daughter in grade school, whom I get ready each morning. I do the meditation and reading before she wakes up because once that happens, she requires my full attention. At night, my time is with my daughter. I most enjoy lying down with her and reading to her. What a different woman than the one who drank every night!

I sponsor just two women right now because I don't like to sponsor a number of people. Sponsoring for me is about guiding you through the steps. I'm not a baby-sitter. I'm not Momma. And I don't want to run people's lives.

I've been married in sobriety, divorced in sobriety, had to leave the state because I was being stalked in sobriety. I recovered from cancer in sobriety. I've had numerous life changes and crises. But I've always been able to go back to center and back to the program to get my spiritual strength. I think it's grace that has kept me sober.

Now, drinking is not an issue for me. Emotional sobriety is what I work toward on a daily basis. Ordinarily, I don't always realize when I'm off center, but I know it when I get around recovering alcoholics. They can see when you're not quite OK with yourself, even when you don't recognize it. I don't know if that explains it very well. When I go into that room, people are real and there are a number of human mirrors to look in. I can see myself with greater clarity and make the necessary adjustments to live a peaceful and contented day.

# 25

## IT'S ALL IN YOUR HEAD

◼

We have seen that some individuals inherit a tendency toward alcohol addiction, but that most people develop the disorder on their own from years of heavy social drinking, made possible by living in a tolerant—and perhaps even encouraging—cultural environment.

If you have a history of the disorder in your family, you might ask, "What exactly have I inherited, and where is it located?"

Or, if you have no such ancestry and have simply altered your own body chemistry by drinking too much for too long, you might wonder, "Just where has that change occurred?"

The place to look is your brain—the source of feelings of pleasure and the origin of the body's demand for *more*.

It has been known for decades that stimulating various parts of our brain with an electrode will cause us to feel thirsty, or hungry, or sexually aroused, depending on where the electrical pulse is applied.[1]

An electrode works because communication within the brain ordinarily occurs when transmitters initiate electrical pulses at nerve endings. One nerve ending will release a neurotransmitter (*neuro* meaning "nerve") into the microscopic gap between nerves, called a "synapse," and the other nerve's receptor will take it up.

Alcohol has been found to affect the neurotransmitters that operate in the pleasure areas of the brain, and any addictive anomalies are likely located there. But where exactly are those areas?

Around 1970, James Olds began mapping the animal brain with an electrode and found a whole bundle of pleasure nerves that, in humans, stretches roughly from behind the ear to the forehead.[2] This appropriately named "reward pathway" runs on a neurotransmitter or communicator known as *dopamine.* Over the years, several other reward pathways have been found, each using a different neurotransmitter. One runs on *serotonin,* another on *gamma-aminobutyric acid* ("GABA"), a third on *opioids.*[3]

By trial and error over the centuries, humans have discovered substances derived from plants and fruits that mimic or enhance the action of the neurotransmitters in these reward pathways. That is why people use a particular substance—to stimulate the pleasure nerve endings. If wooden chairs contained such a substance, millions of people would be walking around chewing on chair legs.

## Dopamine—the Pleasure Transmitter

Dopamine stimulates the nerve receptors in the bundle that forms the primary pleasure pathway in the brain,[4] creating sensations of euphoria, expansion, power, and energy.[5] We know exactly where this nerve bundle is located. It is no surprise to any drinker that alcohol acutely enhances dopamine's affect in the pleasure pathway and other reward centers in the brain.

The bad news is that alcohol may, at times, simply be creating *normal* feelings by temporarily relieving mild underlying anxiety and depression caused by previous drinking.

## Serotonin—the Happiness Transmitter

Serotonin has wonderful effects on us. It reduces depression, alleviates anxiety, elevates mood, and increases feelings of self-worth.[6]

Fact: Autopsies of *alcohol-preferring* animals show that the reward pathways of their brains have abnormally low levels of serotonin.[7]

Fact: Drinking alcohol raises serotonin levels in various areas of the brain.[8]

Question: Is that why alcohol-preferring animals drink—to raise their serotonin level to feel better? If so, *increasing* serotonin activity some other way should cause them to *reduce* their alcohol intake.

To test this theory, scientists artificially stimulated the brain's serotonin receptors in two ways. First, they gave alcohol-preferring rats a drug that emulates serotonin in stimulating its receptors and found, as expected, that the animals voluntarily decreased their alcohol consumption significantly.[9] Next, they gave another group a chemical that intensifies and prolongs the effect of the natural serotonin present in the brain by neutralizing its transponder—a substance in the synapse that "takes up" the serotonin and carries it away after a certain period. In other words, the brain is given an "uptake inhibitor," which attacks serotonin's transportation system in the synapses and gives it more time to stimulate the receptors. By enhancing the activity of the natural serotonin present in the brain, alcohol intake was again markedly lowered.[10]

Apparently, *alcohol-preferring* animals, with low levels of serotonin, do choose to drink more alcohol because their brains lack adequate stimulation from the happiness transmitter.

Behavioral studies conducted on animals[11] indicate that alcohol-preferring *humans,* like laboratory animals, may drink in part to raise their serotonin levels to normal.[12]

But how did the serotonin deficiency originate?

It is possible that certain people are born with a natural deficiency in one or more neurotransmitters or their receptors, causing them to compensate with alcohol or another drug. One study of *alcohol-preferring* rats, in fact, found that they are born with decreased receptor density and reduced serotonin nerve transmission.[13]

But a neurotransmitter deficiency can also be the *result* of alcohol use, rather than its cause. When we artificially stimulate a transmitter system by drinking, our brain recognizes the excess and tries to maintain equilibrium by reducing the production of neurotransmitters and their receptors.[14] We feel the effects of this decrease when sober—by lacking normal feelings of pleasure and happiness—which may lead us to compensate at some point by drinking again. This in turn causes our brain to further reduce the number of transmitters and receptors. The potential for a cycle is created that, when uninterrupted by a period of abstinence, can eventually lead to a need for alcohol just to feel normal.

No wonder that a regular drinker, who has a below-average volume of transmitters chasing a dearth of receptors, can't wait until five o'clock to feel better.

The bad news: Serotonin levels may remain depressed for *up to sixty days* following the beginning of abstinence.[15]

The good news: Once we stay abstinent, our brain seeks equilibrium by naturally increasing the production of neurotransmitters and receptors until we feel good again.

## GABA—the Depressant Transmitter

Most neurotransmitters excite nerve endings. GABA, however, acts as a depressant by occupying receptors and preventing their stimulation. It is the most prevalent neurotransmitter, suppressing the receptivity of nerve endings throughout the brain.

GABA reduces anxiety.[16] Alcohol, a fellow depressant, temporarily enhances its effect.

Unfortunately, our brain likely responds to this artificial dampening by reducing the amount of *natural* depressant. As a result, we feel more stressful or anxious than normal once alcohol leaves our body. People sometimes drink to alleviate these feelings. But then their body reacts with a further reduction of the natural depressant, resulting in more stress and creating the potential for a destructive habit.

Some scientists theorize that we become addicted to alcohol as a stress reducer.[17] As evidence, they note that antianxiety medication markedly reduces the alcohol intake of rats and monkeys.[18] But studies of people *before* they became addicted clearly show that anxiety ordinarily does not precede drinking—it's a *result* of drinking.[19] And that's when it may become the cause of a cycle, which, if perpetuated, can result in addiction.

Others have theorized that depression causes drinking. The truth is that depressed individuals rarely develop addiction, but alcohol-dependent people often become depressed,[20] creating the potential for a situation where a person drinks, feels somewhat depressed the next several days, eventually drinks to be happy, and unwittingly falls into a habit that leads to addiction.

As you would expect, the evidence is overwhelming that abstinence spontaneously relieves both depression and anxiety,[21] including such distressful symptoms of anxiety as occasional heart palpitations and shortness of breath.[22]

## Opioids—the Pain Relief Transmitter

A potential relationship between alcohol and the opiates has long been suspected. In the Victorian era, for example, opiates were prescribed as an effective substitute for an addiction to alcohol. American doctors and British physicians in England, India, and China were convinced that opium eating or smoking by their patients was preferable to the ravages caused by alcohol consumption.[23] At the turn of the century, the Sears Roebuck catalogue listed two pages of drug therapies for morphine addiction and alcoholism—alcohol solutions to treat morphine addiction and tincture of opium for alcoholism.[24] The logic seems bizarre, but they apparently hoped that a person addicted to one would not become dependent on the other.

In 1970, Virginia Davis and Michael Walsh noted the coincidence that alcohol produces the most widespread physical addiction of any substance in the world, while the narcotic morphine alkaloids have the greatest *capacity* for producing physical dependence. Therefore, they suggested that alcohol abuse might be a true addiction involving the production of natural morphine-type alkaloids in the brain—and that the only difference between alcohol and opiate addiction might be "the length of time and dosage required for development of dependence."[25]

Later, natural opiates—such as the endorphins—were indeed discovered in the brain. They suppress pain, relieve stress, and likely induce euphoria, including the "runner's high."[26]

Alcohol activates this natural opioid system, which in turn stimulates a desire for more alcohol.[27] The potential for a cycle is born that, with sporadic stops and starts, can eventually lead to addiction.

Just as a rise in opioid activity prompts an increase in drinking, a *reduction* in opioid activity causes a *decrease* in drinking. This has resulted in a landmark event—the sale of the first new drug for the treatment of alcohol addiction in forty-eight years. It is naltrexone, which *reduces* the ability of opioid transmitters to activate their receptors and is marketed as Revia.™

Patients treated with naltrexone and supportive "don't drink" therapy stay sober for twelve weeks at a rate *three* times that of patients given a placebo.[28] By medically reducing the opioid activity in their brains, these patients experience lower craving for alcohol and drink significantly less if they relapse.[29]

Revia is prescribed for people who need and desire pharmaceutical assistance in gaining a foothold in abstaining from alcohol. Its long-term efficacy is unknown. We shouldn't be too optimistic, however. The brain is so adaptable that the natural course of addiction will not likely be altered by the ingestion of another drug.[30]

## Conclusion

*Don't listen to your mind.* Alcohol addiction is a biochemical disorder of the brain. It involves an imbalance in the neurotransmitter system, which is either genetic in origin or created by excessive drinking. The brain that has become chemically addicted to alcohol is the very organ that is deciding whether you should get into recovery. It's the blind leading the blind. Don't listen to it. Just do what you need to do.[31]

# 26

## DANIEL

■

My secret dream was to save the world by doing something great. In the meantime, I followed the unwritten rule that "everything important in life has to do with money." But no matter what I accomplished or how much I earned, I still needed to drink to get any sense of feeling OK.

Since I found myself depressed much of the time, I recorded what I was thinking, and mostly it was an ongoing "woe is me" chronicle. Looking back, I see that it's the laments of a wounded soul of some kind.

Being self-employed, whenever I got depressed I had the luxury of going around for days in a funk. I might appear normal to you and seem to be functioning, but I wouldn't be doing much, and I'd be drinking a bunch at night. During the day, I'd daydream and wander around in bookstores, searching for answers. I also pursued diversions, such as learning to fly a plane, hoping that they might hold some fulfillment for me. Ultimately, none of those things worked.

I worked as a real estate broker, helping somebody buy or sell. I'd get up every morning and see what deals I had going, what deals I could glue together, and what deals I could start up, and do as much as I could before the day was out.

In thirty years, I went through three booms and busts, each one getting boomier and bustier until the last one busted three decades' worth of work. But I also experienced several periods of dramatic value growth, and assisted people in buying cheap land that made 'em a pile of money. I hit some big licks myself on deals I knew were good, but couldn't sell to anybody else.

During that time, I latched onto drinking beer pretty regular, although I knew it wasn't good for me. I liked the way it made me feel, but I didn't enjoy the aftereffects, and I didn't hanker to being dependent on it. I had never started drinking coffee or smoking cigarettes, so I didn't fancy the idea that I had to have something to be able to feel a certain way.

But I was on an alcohol high.

I didn't need it to go to work or function, but I had to have alcohol sometime before the day was out—to soak up whatever yesterday and today were about. And I was always dreading tomorrow. As long as I was active, it wasn't so bad. But the minute I'd finish what had to be done that day, I'd start worrying about tomorrow, or next year, or the next twenty years.

In retrospect, I recognize that, early in the day, I would start thinking about having a drink. Now, I never did drink during the day. I worked during the day. But I would begin early in the afternoon to determine where I was going to have my first drink—whether at home or some bar—and talk to friends and decide where to meet.

And when I traveled, I knew that the first thing I did after taking care of business was to find a bar. Hotel bar, airport bar, whatever, wherever—gotta find that bar. Now I can see that my drinking was a big part of my thinking. And it remained that way even after it was done. I played handball daily at 6:00 A.M. at the university, and I would get drunk some nights and, oh boy, then get up and play. It served as a penance, with my guilt absolved by the masochistic punishment meted out on the court. And then I'd go sit in the steam room to "sweat out the alcohol." While perspiring profusely, my body would tell me, "Listen, buddy, you can't keep doing this. You either gotta drink—or play handball." Of course, I rationalized that one balanced out the other.

But, drunk or sober, I always felt like a maverick. I didn't fit the world I was in. I functioned in it all right, but I never felt part of it.


In the meantime, my wife and I had five kids, and our ability to spend grew faster than the business. No matter *what* I made, whether lunch money or a truckful, it'd get eaten up—and I had to keep going, doing work that was leaving me empty. Our spending habits also left us without a cushion, so that when the last bust came, we found ourselves in a painful financial bind.

By the time the downturn was full-blown, four of our kids were in high school, and my wife and I were committed to attend everything they did after school—basketball, football, soccer, baseball, drama. I went as an enthusiastic fan, but I also wanted to escape that feeling of impending doom, so I found myself drinking ahead of time and slipping out for beer at intermission. Although I'd be pretty stewed at most events, I believe I conducted myself fine. We were in a religious school atmosphere, so if I hadn't, some do-gooder would likely have come up and said something. But nobody ever told me, "You're acting out of order." Now I suspect that could be because they were afraid of me. During those years, I must have presented a gruff demeanor, because people occasionally asked me what I was mad about, when I wasn't upset at all.

Although I can't identify what I was doing that would make them think that, the best answer, I believe, is that I was an asshole. Of course, when they needed an asshole, there I was. Whenever an unpleasant task arose that nobody wanted to do, I was ready to go. Realtors and builders engaged in a legal battle would come find me because they knew I enjoyed getting in the middle of those; I loved combat and was litigious for many years. I never filed any lawsuits, but I had a bunch filed against me, and I beat 'em—won 'em all. 'Cause I was right, of course!

I rationalized that I was right on principle, grabbed my sword, and charged into the fray. Now I see that entering the fracas is not necessarily right, even if the principle is correct. That's not the best way to solve everything, but that was my nature when I was drinking.

My wife and I have been married twenty-five years, and we've adjusted to each other well over the years. But when that last bust came, I was frustrated all the time, and we had some down-and-dirty word fights. Nothing physical, but some serious cussing and screaming.

When the three-ring circus of money problems, kids, and drinking was entering its grand finale, I had lunch with an old friend whom I'd laid off when the bottom dropped out. We had a good talk, and as we were leaving, I said, "Hey, Brian, let me buy you a drink at the Lakeview Café tonight."

"No thanks, Daniel."

"Well, if you've got other plans . . . I miss seeing you, and I'd like to visit some more. How about Friday at the Cedar Door?"

He hesitated, then leaned forward, elbows on the table, and said, "Dan, I quit drinking."

"Why?"

"I'd appreciate your keeping this confidential, but all those years working for you, I figure I put away a fifth of Scotch almost every night."

"I had no idea."

"Yeah, my wife finally got on me about it. She got tired of raising the kids by herself, while all I did was work and drink."

"How'd you quit?"

"AA."

Several weeks later, I ran into a lawyer friend in a parking lot. I asked him what he was up to, and he said blah, blah, blah—"and by the way, I've joined AA." I had always respected both of those guys, and it gave me pause that they had found a helpful way to deal with alcohol.

I had quit a number of times myself—probably five or six—doing the typical routine where you stop thirty, sixty, or ninety days. I'd get through it and say, "Well, I must not be an alcoholic. I can stop whenever I want." Then I'd go back to it.

But now I decided to give it up for good, and, of course, I still thought that just stopping on my own was the solution.

I quit for about thirty days, then started. Drank a couple of months, then stopped. Thirty days later, something set me off again. On my third try that year, I swore, "If I can't quit by myself this time, I'm going to find one of those AA deals." And, sure enough, it was only a matter of time before I got upset and depressed and just had to have whiskey or beer or something—a bunch of it, quick.

I never liked drinking long hours; I wanted to get that buzz as fast as I could. Typically, I'd hit my favorite bar, have two double bourbons on-the-rocks to get jump-started, then slow down and float on through the evening.

When something set me off that third time, as I was going to the bar, I thought, *I'm gonna do this one, then tomorrow I'm going to AA.* And that's exactly what I did.

I knew the first day that I was exactly where I was supposed to be. I was in a room with people who had been wrestling with the same challenge. Going in, I had that elitist attitude, "I just want some help to stop drinking, but I know I'm not an alcoholic, and I'm sure I'm smarter'n everybody here." But once I heard a few people, I realized I wasn't elite. In fact, I was rather run-of-the-mill when it came to being an alcoholic; I was like a whole bunch of those people, and I was glad to find them.

These were men and women you could talk to about what was *really* going on. Although the whole town was going down the tubes, in the business world you had to keep up a facade: "Oh, I'm doing great! Things are wonderful." You couldn't speak honestly, and I liked being in a place where I didn't have to put up a front and could just say what I thought.

Within three months, I lost the craving for alcohol. But then I saw that my real craving was spiritual. I had been on a spiritual search my whole life, and had investigated many religions—old age, new age, and underage—looking for fulfillment. I adopted their core beliefs, which were all the same, but my actions never matched my spiritual convictions, and that was part of my overall frustration.

What fascinated me about the AA program was that it showed me how to have the spiritual principles become a working part of my life. That was the failing with everything that I had researched—it didn't tell you how.

What I got out of AA was a practice plan. "Go and sin no more," the Bible says. Well, how do you quit doing negative things when they're just habit? So AA gave me a little plan for doing just that. First, I had to recognize when I was in error. Second, when I recognized it, I had to admit it to myself and another human being. Then I had to change—and there's a device for doing that. The religions didn't give me devices for making the change. They just told me to do it.

A great many people can do it on their own. They'll decide, "OK, this is what my faith says to do. I'll just do it," and they can. But not me. I couldn't change on command. I had to have some device for making the switch, and to walk with people who were trying to do the same.

Not a very exciting story. It's kind of routine. But I do think it's probably more common than the low-bottom drunk stories. In the business and middle-class world and up, there's a heck of a lot more alcoholics running around than we ever imagined, and it's affecting many people.

One of my reasons to quit was that, in my family, I could see the "dysfunctional" tension—to use the current buzz word. But it's an accurate description of what goes on in an alcoholic household. Following in my footsteps, the kids had developed a habit of making big issues out of small items. That's a good sign that you're living at Dysfunction Junction—people disagreeing, arguing, and getting in fights over irrelevant things. And avoiding even talking about essential matters.

And in a household of seven people, small irritations are there all the time. Somebody puts their books down, and you move 'em because you want something, and then you have a big argument over, "Well, I put my books there. How come they're not there anymore?" It's amazing how that stuff explodes around the house.

It was unheard of to me, and consequently my kids, that you should not get mad if something happened out of your control. I thought if somebody did something that irritated you, you had every right to get mad. If the sun came up on a day when you wanted rain, or vice versa, you had the right to get angry about that. Well, you have the right, but it's a worthless reaction to an ordinary event. And that's how I define "dysfunction"—people reacting very abnormally to normal things.

What is the cause of that? The best answer I have is that no matter how much you think of yourself as a good person, a hard worker, and somebody willing to sacrifice for your family, in an addictive mode you are not concerned about the other person. You care only about yourself.

And that was me. Even though I did things for my kids, was responsible for them, paid the bills, and went to all their activities, I acted like it was a personal irritation to me when they didn't act grateful about it. Maybe I'd gone all day chasing 'em all over town, doing everything for 'em, and the minute I sat down, one of them would come in and say, "Would you run me over to Joe's house in South Podunk, New Jersey?"

"I've been doing this stuff for you all day," I'd say, pissed off. "Can't you just leave me alone?"

Even though I did it, I acted like it was a burden and pretended to be a martyr. I see that now, but I didn't then. I thought I was this dedicated father who was overburdened, and they ought to say, "Aw, Dad, you do so much for us, take the rest of the night off." And they never said, "Take the rest of the night off." They always said, "Can you do something else?"

Once I was able to change my attitude, I came to the conclusion that it was my job to be a servant to my family—to do things for them that they couldn't do for themselves, and to let them (or make them) do what they were able.

Instead of looking outside my family, thinking I was supposed to do something great in my life and get acknowledged for it, my job was to be the best Daniel that I could and quit worrying about influencing the rest of the world.

When I started to change myself through a recovery program, I began to relate to my family differently. I quit reacting to every little thing they did that I didn't like. I'm sure one of the characteristics of a dysfunctional family is for parents to be overparenting. Every damn thing the kids do, you say something about, or criticize, or try to control. One of the shifts you make is that you quit going to other people, especially your kids, and telling them what's wrong with their lives.

Now I don't tell my kids much unless they ask me. I wait till they come to me and say they've got something troubling them and want advice. At that point, they're open to hearing about my own experience. I've learned from the program not to tell them, "You did that wrong, and you ought to do this instead." There's a world of difference in the way they receive the information when I say, "Well, I understand your situation and I had that problem one time, too. Here's what I did about it. I don't know if it'll work for you."

So I began to let go of control and let them do more things they wanted to do. I tried not to argue with 'em. Just let 'em find out the answers and negative consequences for themselves.

When I began to be less openly concerned about every detail of their lives, the tension level went down. They got more comfortable with me, I got more at ease with them, and my wife and I became more content with each other. All that didn't happen immediately after I let go of control, but there was a gradual and dramatic improvement in the demeanor around our house.

I openly began to confess to my kids that I could see that I was an alcoholic, that it was a dysfunctional way to behave, that whatever the cause of it—genetic or environmental—I had it, and I was accepting that I had it. And I was admitting to them that much of the behavior that resulted from it was not beneficial to them, and that I had channeled their thinking and behavior into the same negative patterns.

When we began to talk about the dysfunctional behavior among us, my kids would say, "Don't mention that word again. We're tired of hearing it."

"We have to discuss it," I said, "because I did my part—I made *you* dysfunctional. But it will be your responsibility to cure it. I can't cure it for you."

But we're all in a recovery frame of mind now. My kids are in college, with three of them still living at home, and we've got many recovery people passing through the house. Their friends and my friends.

Besides family problems that needed to be solved when I got sober, we were also left the financial wreckage of the past. As a success-ful real estate broker for thirty years, I had made an impressive amount of money, but the net result of my entire career was that I had spent more.

Drinking was one of my addictions, but spending money—or, more accurately, spending credit—was another. I didn't know how to deny my family anything, so we lavished money on cars and boats and houses and private schools. And I would spend money just to change my mood. If I felt bad, I'd go buy a new car and feel better for a time. Or go buy a small plane, which I did once and it felt good. You feel like a big shot when you're flying around in your own airplane. But it doesn't last.

One reason I started drinking was that I didn't feel fulfilled, and I didn't feel fulfilled because I didn't feel approval—I didn't feel it from my parents, and then I wanted it from my family and felt that I didn't get it. I later found out that I was getting it but didn't recognize it. I wanted it my way, and when I didn't get it that way, in effect I tried to buy it.

By the time the bust came, I owed more than I made. So I was paralyzed to do anything about it for a time. I've been working on that debt for six years now, operating strictly on a cash basis, and that's been good for me and good for my kids.

When we first went broke, I got them all involved, and said, "Look, we're in a strain here. We've got debts I can't pay. My income is erratic, and y'all need to work part-time and make money. We'll pool our earnings in the family and, on a day-by-day basis, spread it to whoever's got to have it that day. When somebody says, 'I've got to have a tuition payment,' we'll make that payment."

So that's the kind of mode I had to go into in early sobriety—a crisis mode or battlefield mentality: "Here we are. There's nothing we can do about how we got here. We're all gonna have to work together to try to get out, and at the same time we'll hopefully see everybody through college."

I wish that some of that financial wreckage would repair quicker, but something else I learned is that my alcoholic anticipation was always more optimistic than reality. Things just move slower than I believe they ought to. And that's a typical addictive desire—I wanted all the good things fast. I didn't want to muck around with the process. Just give me the result! And now I've learned to enjoy the ride, even though it hasn't been an easy change.


I'm told that when addictive behavior starts, maturity stops. I was twenty-five years old when I began drinking beer with regularity and I didn't begin growing again until I got sober at forty-eight, which left a substantial gap between me and some of my contemporaries.

Although I never thought my drinking was out of line with my compatriots in the business world, looking back, I believe I was worse than most of my peers—but not all of them. I do know some guys who not only went bust financially, but lost their families and everything else, and I don't even know where they are now. On the other hand, many people in the industry went home at night, instead of to the bars.

I'll put it this way. There were a number of people maturing when I wasn't—men and women who were capable and responsible and are retired now. And I, for whatever this combination of drinking and spending and family was, I'm still having to work for a living. When I look around and see contemporaries taking it easy, I realize they made their deal and I didn't.

I no longer want to save the world because it's a whole lot bigger than me, and it's running under some process that I can't identify, in some direction and with certain laws of operation that work all the time, and I'm not gonna change that. To simplify it, my concept of God is that God must be all the energy that's in the universe (and I say "God" just because that's the easiest way to identify it). Exactly what all that is, I don't know, but apparently it's organized and manages to operate perfectly. The only time it appears not to be operating perfectly is when I'm going against it. When I'm in coordination with it, it seems beautiful.

And instead of me trying to manipulate all that, what I've been given is the choice to manipulate *my* behavior—and that's all. So I'm more focused on making myself live in harmony, rather than attempting to force other people to walk to my beat.

I also don't seek out battles anymore, and when presented with one, use humor and patience instead. Plus there are a lot fewer things to clash about than I once thought.

On any day that I'm feeling like I'm not making a contribution to the world, I go to an AA meeting, and if all I do is sit there and listen to somebody, I know I've done my part to help. Even when I don't need the meeting, a man or woman needs me to be there to listen. I used to beat myself up because I wasn't saving the world, and I could do that bad enough to take a drink. Well, I don't have to do that now—all I have to do is be of service to someone else.

# 27

## WHERE BLINDNESS LEADS

A lcohol addiction is so common, and so harmful to the body, that fully 25 percent of the people admitted to general hospitals are addicted.[1] So are 20 percent of patients at private medical clinics.[2] Extraordinary, isn't it?

Yet, equally extraordinary, doctors fail to identify nine out of ten of these alcoholic patients.[3] Why? Because most drinkers underestimate their consumption by *half*,[4] and the heavier the drinking, the greater the error. In fact, the heaviest drinkers actually consume *three times as much as they say.*[5] Just as many obese people always claim to be dieting or eating moderately, alcohol abusers often claim to "drink socially," averaging merely a couple of drinks a day.[6]

The deception ordinarily is not intentional—these drinkers are in unconscious denial, to themselves as much as to their doctor—but the result is that addiction to alcohol is rarely treated professionally.

In the meantime, the individual may suffer a host of seemingly unrelated physical consequences. Let's look at them.

### The Heart

Alcoholism immediately brings to mind the liver, but in fact it kills *mainly through its impact on the heart muscle,* with cardiovascular disease alone causing one of every three deaths. Because the heart is so vulnerable, shortness of breath or benign heart palpitations are found to occur in some addicted men.[7]

Although many studies have "documented the contribution of alcohol abuse to left ventricular cardiac dysfunction, arrhythmias, and heart failure,"[8] the general public is still in the dark about the significant association between alcohol abuse and heart disease. We shake our heads in disbelief when a person with a cardiac disorder persists in drinking, failing to realize that the heart ailment may well have been caused by alcohol in the first place.

## The Big C

After heart disease, cancer is the greatest killer of men and women addicted to alcohol. Even if you eliminate the smokers and obese people, fully *half* of their premature deaths are caused by heart disease and cancer. In comparison, only 2 percent die from cirrhosis.[9]

## The Ominous Threat of Epidemic

Drinking alcohol suppresses the body's normal immune response to bacteria and viruses. *People who use alcohol to excess— either occasionally or regularly—are immunosuppressed,* and thus subject to more frequent and more severe infections. They don't respond well to treatment and have a striking vulnerability to pneumonia and tuberculosis.[10]

The death rate for men with pneumonia who are addicted to alcohol is three times the normal rate. Women die seven times more often than expected.[11] But these numbers may worsen rapidly because many bacterial strains are fast becoming resistant to antibiotics, and individuals abusing alcohol may unexpectedly find themselves in still graver danger.

Consider this: As recently as 1987, only 0.02 percent of streptococcus pneumonia in the U.S.A. was resistant to penicillin. By 1995, according to a study conducted by the Center for Disease

Control (CDC), that minuscule percentage had jumped to an alarming 25 percent in Atlanta. That's a thousandfold increase, indicating a potentially catastrophic spread in drug-resistant germs.[12]

Streptococcus is annually responsible for half a million cases of pneumonia, six thousand cases of meningitis, and perhaps six million inner-ear infections—in the U.S.A. alone.[13] Worldwide, this organism causes three to five million deaths a year.

The CDC study showed that the highest percentage of drug-resistant strains, 41 percent, was among white children younger than six years of age. Black children had a 20 percent rate.[14]

*The New England Journal of Medicine,* in a 1995 article titled "The Pneumococcus at the Gates," called the numbers "astonishing" and "a chilling reminder that the United States is no longer safe from the spread of penicillin-resistant and multidrug-resistant" bacteria, which are already prevalent in Spain, Hungary, and parts of Africa and South America.[15] This normally staid medical journal pleads, "We need novel antibacterial agents urgently."[16]

A similar spread of drug-resistant tuberculosis is occurring. In New York City, its presence in people who had never been treated for TB more than doubled—from 10 percent to 23 percent—between 1984 and 1991. This explosion of drug-resistant strains in just seven years is particularly frightening because no increase whatsoever had occurred nationally in the United States since 1950.[17]

Contracting a drug-resistant TB strain is serious business, requiring a hospital stay averaging seven months, with almost half the patients failing to recover.[18] The medical specialists trying to save them recently declared:

> If we, with all our resources, can successfully
> treat less than 60 percent of such patients,
> what will happen in less ideal circumstances?[19]

People addicted to alcohol are particularly susceptible to contracting tuberculosis. In 1992, 42 percent of the patrons in a Minneapolis neighborhood bar contracted the disease from a fellow customer.[20]

In sum, the threat of drug-resistant strains of pneumonia and tuberculosis is ominous and poses a major danger to people who are immunosuppressed from excessive use of alcohol.

## There's Nothing Worse Than an Airhead

Since alcoholism is a disorder of the brain, it's no surprise that perhaps one-third to one-half of all test patients with long-term alcohol dependence have shown abnormal brain-scan results. The ventricles—the empty spaces in the brain that extend from the spinal canal—were enlarged from abuse. In other words, as the surrounding brain matter is destroyed, the brain shrinks and the cavities grow bigger.[21]

This shrinkage is not limited to older people. Almost half of those in their twenties show changes in the cortex after five years of very heavy drinking.[22]

## Unless it's an Anxious Airhead

Almost one in three alcoholics suffers from persistent worry, depression, anxiety, or occasional panic attacks.[23] Tragically, many women in this situation receive antianxiety or antidepressant medication because doctors and nurses fail to recognize these symptoms as hallmarks of female alcohol abuse.

For women and men addicted to alcohol, abstinence almost always relieves these symptoms.

## Strokes

Among men averaging four or more drinks a day, the risk of stroke is *four times* that in nondrinkers. Perhaps this is caused by a direct constriction of the blood vessels in the brain, which might explain strokes suffered during binge drinking.[24] Women who average three or more drinks a day also have a significantly increased risk of stroke.[25]

## Hepatitis C

The effect of alcohol abuse on the liver is well known. What is less known is that Hepatitis C essentially renders the liver defenseless to alcohol, and this combination has been killing unsuspecting people.

## No Wonder So Many Urinals Have Cigarette Butts

Drinking causes nicotine addicts to smoke more. Since alcohol speeds the elimination of nicotine through the urine, more cigarettes are required to maintain the normal nicotine blood levels.[26]

Other people poison their bodies with smoking only while drinking, either because of poor judgment caused by intoxication or to offset the depressant effects of alcohol with a nicotine boost.

## Where's That Nonsmoking Meeting?

Heavy smoking shortens life by eight years. Long-term alcohol abuse is twice as lethal, reducing longevity by fifteen years.[27]

One study of 500 men addicted to alcohol showed they died at *an average age of fifty-two.* Tragically, many of them quit drinking for long periods of time, only to relapse at some later point.[28]

And here's a tremendous incentive for men and women in recovery to surrender their nicotine addiction: Heavy smokers who successfully quit drinking continue to die at twice the normal rate—the same as their colleagues who never stopped abusing alcohol.[29]

In 1996, a medical research group reported that more than *half* of the deceased graduates of an inpatient treatment program had died from tobacco-related diseases.[30] As a result, these doctors issued an emphatic call for treatment of nicotine dependence in the recovery community.

Although some treatment centers continue to ignore nicotine addiction, fearful of asking too much of their clients at once, others are discovering that—for people who are willing—nicotine dependence can be treated successfully without interfering with abstinence from alcohol and other drugs.[31]

# 28

## WHAT CAN I DO?

You have come to a time when it is no longer necessary,
nor is it possible, to continue to go it alone.

—anonymous

We've made great strides in our knowledge about the human
brain. In fact, 80 percent of all we know has been learned
in just the last twelve years. But our present knowledge doesn't
even hint at a solution to the scientific puzzle of alcohol addiction.

The future may reveal the precise mechanism by which excessive consumption or genetic predisposition results in distorted
brain chemistry, along with medication to correct the self-induced
imbalance or complex gene therapy to remove and replace any
abnormal genes.[1]

In the meantime, most "medical" treatment consists of a detox-
ifying abstinence, followed by education, support, and counseling, whether as an "inpatient" in a residential setting or as an
"outpatient" who attends evening sessions while continuing to
work and live at home.

Because many people can't afford treatment, the vast majority
who recover luckily manage to do so without professional care.

Let's briefly survey the options that are out there.

## Controlled-Drinking Training

The first cure that most of us try is controlled drinking.

But as millions have learned on their own, it doesn't work. In fact, teaching controlled-drinking skills in a formal training program can actually backfire. In the first six months following training, it ironically can lead to more abuse and less abstinence than if no such "training" had occurred.[2]

Over the long term, controlled-drinking training has no impact whatsoever.[3]

## Shrinks

Persistent low-level depression, worry, or stress—all caused or exacerbated by alcohol—drives many drinkers to seek counseling for their symptoms. Others land on the therapist's couch due to relationship problems or the pain of divorce.

Often, neither patient nor therapist realizes that alcohol is the root of the problem. Both assume that if childhood or personality issues are faced and resolved, any excessive drinking will vanish spontaneously.

As a result, psychotherapy historically has been an overwhelming failure in helping abusers become abstinent.[4] *Ironically, therapy may, in fact, pose an obstacle to achieving* initial *sobriety.* By searching for mythical psychological causes of alcohol abuse, patients frequently fail to recognize their addiction, which may simply be biochemical.[5]

As with cigarettes, an addiction to alcohol isn't just an emotional or intellectual problem.

Studies show that psychotherapy is often less effective than using self-help materials—particularly for women—unless the therapist has many years of experience in counseling persons with alcohol or drug problems.[6]

Once someone has stopped drinking, however, therapy can be very beneficial in assisting a person in staying sober. Emotions that trigger a desire for alcohol, such as anger or loneliness, can now be explored with relative clarity. And the subconscious needs previously satisfied by drinking can be identified and fulfilled by other means.

Most importantly, those of us who have anesthetized our true feelings with alcohol for many years can use all the assistance we can find in learning how to live a contented and joy-filled life. The luxury of a personal, professional adviser once was available only to royalty. Why not take advantage of it now?

## Inpatient Treatment

In recent years, many companies have instituted employee assistance programs, with billions of health insurance dollars spent annually on inpatient treatment.

Such treatment programs once were notoriously ineffective. In 1974, for example, a respected researcher found that "alcoholics are, in a practical sense, as likely to stop drinking completely for six months or longer when they have no [treatment]."[7]

But the efficacy of treatment has improved tremendously of late. Today, more than half of those who complete a quality inpatient treatment program are sober during the fourth year after graduation.[8] Most who relapse do so in the first year—many within days of treatment—because they don't take advantage of a mutual support group.

The length of treatment required varies by individual. Some men and women are released to outpatient care after seven days; others need the structure, privacy, and intensity of a four-week program. Even those in the worst imaginable circumstances have a better-than-even chance of achieving stable abstinence and employment with extended treatment.[9]

Numerous excellent treatment centers are available at a relatively reasonable cost. At a few, the charge for inpatient care borders on criminality. Some of the worst programs charge four times more than the best. So shop around for quality and price. The cost of an airline ticket may be the cheapest and best investment you ever made.

## Day Clinics

A less expensive alternative eliminates the cost of room and board. Patients attend treatment full time during the day and go home at night and on weekends. For some, the success rate is comparable to inpatient treatment, while saving 60 percent of the cost.[10] And because it eliminates the transition back into the home environment, most patients express a greater sense of well-being the first six months after discharge.[11]

A word of caution: Selecting a less intensive regimen solely for financial reasons may turn out to be a foolish choice, given the cost of a destructive lifestyle.

## Evening Treatment

Severely addicted persons and connoisseurs of more than one drug—including alcohol—ordinarily need inpatient treatment. So do people whose social support structure has been destroyed. They can hardly be expected to turn their lives around without an intensive program.[12]

But for others, a brief intervention combined with a comprehensive outpatient treatment program is an attractive alternative. It not only costs less, but its success rate can be as good as residential care.[13]

## The Pain Treatment Program

Many people recover without treatment—often on the condition that they suffer severe enough pain. For some, the humiliation of being inebriated in front of their wide-eyed child is enough to stop. Others quit when their beloved spouse packs to leave. Many reform when threatened with the loss of their livelihood. But most continue to spiral downward, searching for a bottom short of death.

Regrettably, well-intentioned family members and friends, or faithful employees, frequently blunt the impact of the painful repercussions that can lead to recovery. The appalling truth is that such loving assistance enables the addict to continue drinking.[14]

If you are concerned about someone you love, rather than be an unwitting accomplice, try attending a few meetings of an Al-Anon Family Group, where friends and relatives of people addicted to alcohol share their experience, strength, and hope. Another excellent alternative is to seek a loving intervention through competent professional help. Its purpose is to assist the drinker to see reality, to accomplish that with respect, and to offer hopeful options that can be accepted with dignity.[15]

## Man, I Want Another Drug

Rapid advances in our understanding of the biochemical interaction between alcohol and the brain will likely lead to the sale of numerous compounds to assist addicted men and women in the initial stages of recovery. As noted earlier, one drug affecting the opioid system has already been found effective.

We may soon see a flood of neurotransmitter enhancers, antagonists, and uptake inhibitors targeting serotonin, GABA, dopamine, the endorphins, and their receptors.

It is dangerous that the very industry that flooded us with tranquilizers and antidepressants now intends to profitably guide us to pharmaceutical nirvana. The current journals in psychiatry all have full-page ads trumpeting miracle drugs that relieve depression, anxiety, and insomnia—medications that inevitably will be mistakenly prescribed simply to alleviate the withdrawal symptoms of alcohol abuse. The pill dispensers are alive and well.

But ultimately, hope may lie in this direction for millions of people. The brutal fact is that the overwhelming number of alcoholics now actively suffer with the disorder until they die. A nondestructive medical alternative would be welcomed by all.

## A Proven and Free Solution

A statistically proven solution to alcohol addiction is available today, when we decide to do something about our drinking *and* seek support from people who have walked the same path and are living happy, sober lives.

In 1935 a stockbroker and a surgeon, both with a Ph.D. in drinking, founded a mutual-support organization, Alcoholics Anonymous, which has been so successful that attendance in many communities has become a source of pride rather than a stigma.

Studies show that voluntary AA involvement is a significant predictor of sobriety—attendance mandated by a judge or employer has poor results. And the greater the voluntary participation, the longer the sobriety.[16]

AA's success rate increases with time. The odds of an *active* member staying sober one more year improves from 40 percent during the first year of sobriety to 80 percent in years two to five, and 90 percent after year five.[17]

Most strikingly, *men and women who assist newcomers by serving as their mentor have a 91 percent remission rate.*[18] No wonder that helping others is the foundation of the program.

The best evidence of its efficacy is that AA, a group once composed of Anglo middle-aged, male smokers, has found its membership exploding worldwide among women and the young. Almost two-thirds of AA members live outside the U.S., with countries such as Costa Rica and El Salvador having twice as many AA groups per capita.[19]

A listed phone number can be found for the local Alcoholics Anonymous group in virtually every city in the United States, as well as in major metropolitan areas around the world. In fact, most cities have numerous AA groups because all it takes to start a new one is a recovering alcoholic with a resentment toward the old group, a coffeepot, and a Big Book. Since each group has its own distinctive personality, I strongly recommend shopping several to find the one where you feel most comfortable. Certainly don't decide the AA program is not for you based on a single meeting at one group. That's like reading a random page of a great author's work.

## Other Mutual-Support Groups

Active involvement in any group where drinking is not the norm can result in sustained abstinence because of the reinforcement gained from shared attitudes and values.[20] Many find it through active participation in their church community; others, through a social network of nondrinking friends and family. In addition, nonspiritually based recovery groups, such as Women for Sobriety, Secular Organizations for Sobriety (SOS), and S.M.A.R.T. Recovery can be found in a growing number of communities.* But the reality is that, for most people, the transition out of a lifestyle of addicted drinking needs to be jump-started with treatment, AA, or both.

## Conclusion

Whether you choose inpatient treatment, evening classes, AA, or another support group, *do something.* And don't do it alone. Go somewhere and talk to people. Stop letting your addicted brain be your sole consultant because it will always reach one conclusion: "I could quit, but I won't"—which is just another way of saying *you can't.*[21]

---

*The "New Life" Acceptance Program of Women for Sobriety is set out in the appendix, as is its contact information, that of SOS, and S.M.A.R.T. Recovery.

# 29

## THINKING PERSON'S TEST

◼

Because no two people are identical in their addiction to alcohol, a definitive diagnosis would require a lengthy and honest dialogue with a skilled interviewer. However, a ten-minute self-administered test is useful as a quick barometer for someone wondering if it would be reasonable to explore the issue by attending a few AA meetings, most of which are open to nonalcoholic visitors and whose *only* requirement for membership is "a desire to stop drinking."

The following areas of inquiry are apparent from various sources in the scientific literature, as well as from personal observation and experience.[1]

Write "Yes" or "No" after each question:

1. Do you ever fail to remember things that happened while you were drinking?

2. Does your hand ever shake in the morning after drinking?

3. Do you drink more heavily when depressed, under pressure, or anxious?

4. Do you regularly drink to relieve anger, insomnia, or fatigue?

5. Are you annoyed when someone criticizes your drinking?

6. Do you ever drink, or take a prescription drug, to relieve a hangover?

7. When someone pours you a glass of wine, do you secretly compare the level of liquid in your glass to that poured for others around the table?

8. Do you periodically feel remorseful about your drinking?

9. Have you tried switching drinks or following different plans to limit your drinking?

10. Do you periodically neglect your obligations at work, school, or home because of drinking or hangovers?

11. Are there occasions when you feel uncomfortable because alcohol is not available?

12. Have you ever been arrested for behavior while you were drinking, such as drinking and driving, public intoxication, or disturbing the peace?

13. Do you regularly drink to be more appealing or to relieve shyness, boredom, or loneliness?

14. Have you stopped drinking for a time to prove you can?

15. Do you impatiently, or lovingly, anticipate having your first drink of the day?

16. Do you sometimes drink while driving home from school or work, or while driving on a long trip?

17. Have you found that you have increased the number, size, or strength of your drinks since you first started drinking?

18. Do you regret things you've said or done while drinking?

19. Do you regularly fail to keep promises to yourself about your drinking?

20. Are you concerned that you might have a drinking problem?

*If you have skipped the test to check the scoring system that follows, take the test first to avoid invalidating your own results.*

As a thinking person, you know that any "Yes" answer deserves reflection. You may already have decided to explore the issue further, which is wise if you are concerned that you might have a drinking problem. If you answered "Yes" to three or more of these questions, it would certainly be reasonable to attend a few support group meetings, consult a psychotherapist experienced in alcohol and drug counseling, or obtain a confidential assessment from a qualified professional at an alcohol clinic.

## EPILOGUE

There is every reason for you or your loved one to land as quickly and as high as possible. Life is short. Unfortunately, when the alcohol addict finally hits bottom and begins living again, years have passed irretrievably—years in which children have grown, their precious childhoods missed; years in which loved ones have left to spend their lives with others; years in which beauty and good health have gradually faded or been unknowingly destroyed; years in which numerous days that could have been lived without stress in a world filled with sunshine and smiles instead were squandered in a quiet, desperate, physical, and emotional struggle.

Let today be your "sobriety birthday," and from *this* moment forward:

> Look to this day,
> For it is life,
> The very life of life.
> In its brief course lie all
> The realities and verities of existence,
> The bliss of growth,
> The splendor of action,
> The glory of power.
>
> For yesterday is but a dream,
> And tomorrow is only a vision,
> But today, well lived,
> Makes every yesterday a dream of happiness
> And every tomorrow a vision of hope.
>
> Look well, therefore, to this day.

*—Sanskrit Proverb*

# POSTSCRIPT

◩

O n almost every scientific subject covered in this book, various schools of thought exist. The information presented could not be "exhaustive" without having the same effect on the reader, and that means choices were made. The predominant scientific view, if any, is often reported, and I was certainly influenced by my personal research on alcoholism, which most scientists luckily did not conduct. I know you don't have to suffer from cancer to be a good oncologist, but there's no objective test for the amorphous disorder we call alcoholism, and years of personal experience do afford some insight.

Mistakes are inevitable in attempting to summarize several fields of research, but hopefully all will gracefully turn out to be minor.

Also, many of the facts are subject to modification as new research is conducted; and geneticists, brain specialists, epidemiologists, and others are publishing scores of new articles each month.

# APPENDIX

## The Twelve Steps of Alcoholics Anonymous

1. We admitted we were powerless over alcohol—that our lives had become unmanageable.

2. Came to believe that a Power greater than ourselves could restore us to sanity.

3. Made a decision to turn our will and our lives over to the care of God *as we understood Him.*

4. Made a searching and fearless moral inventory of ourselves.

5. Admitted to God, to ourselves, and to another human being the exact nature of our wrongs.

6. Were entirely ready to have God remove all these defects of character.

7. Humbly asked Him to remove our shortcomings.

8. Made a list of all persons we had harmed, and became willing to make amends to them all.

9. Made direct amends to such people wherever possible, except when to do so would injure them or others.

10. Continued to take personal inventory and when we were wrong promptly admitted it.

11. Sought through prayer and meditation to improve our conscious contact with God, *as we understood Him,* praying only for knowledge of His will for us and the power to carry that out.

12. Having had a spiritual awakening as the result of these steps, we tried to carry this message to alcoholics, and to practice these principles in all our affairs.

The Twelve Steps are reprinted with permission of Alcoholics Anonymous World Services, Inc. Permission to reprint the Twelve Steps does not mean that AA has reviewed or approved the contents of this publication, nor that AA agrees with the views expressed herein. AA is a program of recovery from alcoholism *only*—use of the Twelve Steps in connection with programs and activities which are patterned after AA, but which address other problems, or in any other non–AA context, does not imply otherwise.

For more information on Alcoholics Anonymous, write the AA General Service Office, 475 Riverside Drive, New York, NY 10015, or call (212) 870-3400. The home page for AA on the World Wide Web at "www.alcoholics-anonymous.org/" contains the address and phone number of the local general service office for countries throughout the world.

## "New Life" Acceptance Program of Women for Sobriety, Inc.

1. I have a drinking (life-threatening) problem that once had me. *I now take charge of my life and my disease. I accept the responsibility.*

2. Negative thoughts destroy only myself.
   *My first conscious sober act must be to remove negativity from my life.*

3. Happiness is a habit I will develop.
   *Happiness is created, not waited for.*

4. Problems bother me only to the degree I permit them to.
   *I now better understand my problems and do not permit problems to overwhelm me.*

5. I am what I think.
   *I am a capable, competent, caring, compassionate woman.*

6. Life can be ordinary or it can be great.
   *Greatness is mine by a conscious effort.*

7. Love can change the course of my world.
   *Caring becomes all important.*

8. The fundamental object of life is emotional and spiritual growth.
   *Daily I put my life into a proper order, knowing which are the priorities.*

9. The past is gone forever.
   *No longer will I be victimized by the past. I am a new person.*

10. All love given returns.
    *I will learn to know that others love me.*

11. Enthusiasm is my daily exercise.
    *I treasure all moments of my new life.*

12. I am a competent woman and have much to give life.
    *This is what I am and I shall know it always.*

13. I am responsible for myself and for my actions.
    *I am in charge of my mind, my thoughts, and my life.*

Women for Sobriety, Inc., was founded in 1976 by Dr. Jean Kirkpatrick, who was influenced by the writings of Ralph Waldo

Emerson and other metaphysical writers. For more information, send a self-addressed, stamped business-size envelope to WFS, P.O. Box 618, Quakertown, PA 18951-0618, or call (215) 536-8026. The organization also has a home page on the World Wide Web at "www.media pulse.com/wfs/" and can be reached by E-mail at "wfsobriety @aol.com".

## Secular Organizations for Sobriety

Also known as Save Our Selves, SOS seeks to promote sobriety as an alternative recovery method for those who are uncomfortable with the spiritual content of twelve-step programs. It began in 1985 with an article in *Free Inquiry* magazine, the leading secular humanist journal in the United States. SOS is a subcommittee of the Council for Secular Humanism, and can be contacted by writing SOS National Clearinghouse, The Center for Inquiry–West, 5521 Grosvenor Boulevard, Los Angeles, CA 90066, or by calling (310) 821-8430. SOS also has a home page on the World Wide Web at "www.secularhumanism.org/sos/".

## S.M.A.R.T. Recovery

Self-management and Recovery Training (S.M.A.R.T.) uses rational emotive behavioral therapy devised by psychologist Albert Ellis to encourage and support abstinence. The program emphasizes:

1. Enhancing motivation.
2. Refusing to act on urges to use.
3. Managing life's problems in a sensible and effective way without substances.
4. Developing a positive, balanced, and healthy lifestyle.

S.M.A.R.T. Recovery can be reached at 24000 Mercantile Road, Suite 11, Beachwood, Ohio 44122, or by calling (216) 292-0220. The organization also has a home page on the World Wide Web at "www.smartrecovery.org/" and can be reached by E-mail at "srmail/1@aol.com."

# NOTES

◾

## CHAPTER 6: LIE DOWN ON YOUR BACK AND YELL, "UNCLE!"

1. *Alcoholics Anonymous,* 3d ed. (New York: Alcoholics Anonymous World Services, 1976), 570 (italics in original).
2. Ibid., 28.

## CHAPTER 10: WIND CHIMES

1. See note 1, chap. 6, 83–4 (emphasis added).

## CHAPTER 11: WHO ARE THE ALCOHOLICS AMONG US?

1. "Epidemiology of Alcohol Abuse and Alcoholism," chap. 1 in the Fifth Special Report to the U.S. Congress on Alcohol and Health. U.S. Department of Health and Human Services (NIAAA). (Washington, D.C.: U.S. Government Printing Office, 1983).
2. Marc A. Schuckit, M.D., *Drug and Alcohol Abuse: A Clinical Guide to Diagnosis and Treatment,* 4th ed., (New York: Plenum Publishing, 1995), 80–83.
3. Ibid., 82–83.
4. "Epidemiology of Alcohol Use and Alcohol-Related Consequences," chap. 1 in the Eighth Special Report to the U.S. Congress on Alcohol and Health. U.S. Department of Health and Human Services (NIAAA). (Washington, D.C.: U.S. Government Printing Office, 1993), 41.
5. See note 2, chap. 11, page 83.
6. George E. Vaillant, M.D., *The Natural History of Alcoholism Revisited* (Cambridge: Harvard University Press, 1995), 199–200.
7. See note 2, chap. 11, page 83.
8. Marc A. Schuckit, M.D. et al., "The Time Course of Develop-

ment of Alcohol-Related Problems in Men and Women," *Journal of Studies on Alcohol* 56 (1995): 222.

9. See note 2, chap. 11, pages 59, 97.

10. Ibid., 101.

11. Ibid., 102, 112.

12. Harold L. Williams and O. H. Rundell, Jr., "Altered Sleep Physiology in Chronic Alcoholics: Reversal with Abstinence," *Alcoholism: Clinical and Experimental Research* 5 (1981): 318–25.

13. C. Robert Cloninger et al., "Effects of Changes in Alcohol Use Between Generations on Inheritance of Alcohol Abuse," in *Alcoholism: Origins and Outcome,* edited by Robert M. Rose, M.D., and James E. Barrett, M.D. (New York: Raven Press, 1988), 55.

14. John E. Helzer, M.D., and Glorisa J. Canino, "Comparative Analysis of Alcoholism in Ten Cultural Regions," *Alcoholism in North America, Europe, and Asia* (New York: Oxford University Press, 1992), 303.

15. See note 13, chap. 11, page 58.

## CHAPTER 13: GRANDPA MADE ME

1. Roger J. Williams, *The Prevention of Alcoholism Through Nutrition* (New York: Bantam Books, 1981), 23.

2. Leonora Mirone, "The Effect of Ethyl Alcohol on Growth, Fecundity and Voluntary Consumption of Alcohol by Mice," *Quarterly Journal of Studies on Alcoholism* 13 (1952): 365–69.

3. Jorge Mardones R., M.D., "On the Relationship Between Deficiency of B Vitamins and Alcohol Intake in Rats," *Quarterly Journal of Studies on Alcoholism* 12 (1951): 563–75; Jorge Mardones R., M.D., Natividad Segovia M., and Arturo Hederra D., M.D., "Heredity of Experimental Alcohol Preference in Rats: II. Coefficient of Heredity," *Quarterly Journal of Studies on Alcoholism* 14 (1953): 1–2.

4. Nada J. Estes and M. Edith Heinemann, *ALCOHOLISM: development, consequences, and interventions,* 3d ed. (St. Louis: C.V. Mosby, 1986), 23.

5. Donald W. Goodwin, M.D. et al., "Alcohol Problems in Adoptees Raised Apart From Alcoholic Biological Parents," *Archives of General Psychiatry* 28 (1973): 238–43. The risk factor is probably

even greater, not only because of the young age of the sample, but also because the control group of "normal" children likely contained kids whose parents were alcoholic but who had never been hospitalized for the disorder, which was the definition of parental alcoholism used in the study.

6. See note 13, chap. 11, page 65.

7. Ibid., 60–64.

8. See note 5, chap. 13, page 240.

9. See note 6, chap. 11, page 67.

10. See note 5, chap. 13, page 239.

11. See note 6, chap. 11, page 220.

12. George E. Vaillant, "Some Differential Effects of Genes and Environment on Alcoholism," in *Alcoholism: Origins and Outcome,* edited by Robert M. Rose, M.D., and James E. Barrett, M.D. (New York: Raven Press, 1988), 77.

13. Ibid., 78–80; Donald W. Goodwin, M.D., "Alcoholism: Who Gets Better and Who Does Not," in *Alcoholism: Origins and Outcome,* edited by Robert M. Rose, M.D., and James E. Barrett, M.D. (New York: Raven Press, 1988), 281–92.

14. Donald W. Goodwin, M.D., *Is Alcoholism Hereditary?* (New York: Oxford University Press, 1976).

15. Nancy S. Cotton, "The Familial Incidence of Alcoholism," *Journal of Studies on Alcohol* 40 (1979): 89–116.

16. See note 6, chap. 11, page 74.

17. Ibid., 75.

18. Lennart Kaij, *Alcoholism in Twins* (Stockholm: Almqvist and Wiksell, 1960), 35–36.

19. See note 6, chap. 11, pages 46–52; see note 13, chap. 13, page 283.

20. Persons with normal personality tests (MMPI) in college were found to have tests typical of alcoholics after developing the addiction. M. L. Kammeier, H. Hoffman, and R. G. Loper, "Personality Characteristics of Alcoholics as College Freshmen and at Time of Treatment," *Quarterly Journal of Studies on Alcoholism* 34 (1973): 390–99. They had become the self-centered, immature, and resentful people we've come to expect. R. G. Loper, M. L. Kammeier, and H. Hoffmann, "M.M.P.I. Characteristics of College Freshman Males Who Later Became Alcoholics," *Journal of*

*Abnormal Psychology* 82 (1973): 159–62. However, the occasional individual does have a primary psychiatric disorder with only secondary alcoholism, and it will be necessary for that person to seek professional psychiatric care.

21. Stephen F. A. Elston et al., "Ethanol Intoxication as a Function of Genotype Dependent Responses in Three Inbred Mice Strains," *Pharmacology, Biochemistry & Behavior* 16 (1982): 13–15.

22. Marc A. Schuckit, M.D., "Subjective Responses to Alcohol in Sons of Alcoholics and Control Subjects," *Archives of General Psychiatry* 41 (1984): 879–84.

23. Marc A. Schuckit, M.D., "Low Level of Response to Alcohol as a Predictor of Future Alcoholism," *American Journal of Psychiatry* 151 (1994): 184–89.

24. Kenneth Blum and James E. Payne, *Alcohol and the Addictive Brain* (New York: Free Press, 1991), 223.

25. See note 6, chap. 11, page 70.

26. Henri Begleiter et al., "Event-Related Brain Potentials in Boys at Risk for Alcoholism," *Science* 225 (1984): 1493–96.

27. Shirley Y. Hill and Stuart R. Steinhauer, "Assessment of Prepubertal and Postpubertal Boys and Girls at Risk for Developing Alcoholism with P300 from a Visual Discrimination Task," *Journal of Studies on Alcohol* 54 (1993): 350–58; Stuart R. Steinhauer and Shirley Y. Hill, "Auditory Event-Related Potentials in Children at High Risk for Alcoholism," *Journal of Studies on Alcohol* 54 (1993): 408–21; Shirley Y. Hill et al., "P300 Amplitude Decrements in Children from Families of Alcoholic Female Probands," *Biological Psychiatry* 38 (1995): 622–32.

28. Shirley Y. Hill and Stuart R. Steinhauer, "Event-Related Potentials in Women at Risk for Alcoholism," *Alcohol* 10 (1993): 349–54.

## CHAPTER 15: I'VE GOT THE BOMB, WHEN DOES IT EXPLODE?

1. See note 6, chap. 11, pages 69 and 103.

2. See note 12, chap. 13, pages 78–80.

3. Marc A. Schuckit, M.D. et al., "Increases in Alcohol-Related Problems for Men on a College Campus between 1980 and 1992," *Journal of Studies on Alcohol* 55 (1994): 739–42. Although total consumption declined in the 1980s, a significant increase in

alcohol-related problems occurred among young single people, particularly women and students, and among Hispanics. Lorraine T. Midanik and Walter B. Clark, "Drinking-Related Problems in the United States: Description and Trends, 1984–1990," *Journal of Studies on Alcohol* 56 (1995): 397–98. Young people aged eighteen to twenty-nine drank less as a group, but showed a 50 percent increase in problem drinking. Ibid., 398, 400.

4. Henry Wechsler and Nancy Isaac, " 'Binge' Drinkers at Massachusetts Colleges: Prevalence, Drinking Style, Time Trends, and Associated Problems," *Journal of the American Medical Association* 267 (1992): 2929–31.

5. Kaye M. Fillmore, Seiden D. Bacon, and Merton Hyman, "The 27 Year Longitudinal Panel Study of Drinking by Students in College, 1949–76," Final Report. NIAAA Contract No. ADM 231-76-0015 (1979), 524–25.

6. Ibid., 502–03, 524.

7. Kaye M. Fillmore and Lorraine Midanik, "Chronicity of Drinking Problems among Men: A Longitudinal Study," *Journal of Studies on Alcohol* 45 (1984): 231.

8. See note 5, chap. 15, pages 456–58, 505, 527 (emphasis added).

9. Richard S. DeFrank, C. David Jenkins, and Robert M. Rose, M.D., "A Longitudinal Investigation of the Relationships Among Alcohol Consumption, Psychosocial Factors, and Blood Pressure," *Psychosomatic Medicine* 49 (1987): 236–49; Martin A. Plant, *Drinking Careers: Occupations, Drinking Habits, and Drinking Problems* (London: Tavistock, 1979), 133.

10. Ibid., *Drinking Careers.*

11. See note 7, chap. 15, pages 228–36.

12. See note 5, chap. 15, page 506.

13. See note 6, chap. 11, page 166.

## CHAPTER 17: WAKE-UP CALL FOR WOMEN

1. "Substance Abuse and the American Woman," The National Center on Addiction and Substance Abuse at Columbia University (June, 1996); "Effects of Alcohol on Health and Body Systems," chap. 8 in the Eighth Special Report to the U.S. Congress on Alcohol and Health. U.S. Department of Health and Human Services (NIAAA). (Washington, D.C.: U.S. Government Printing Office,

1993); Arthur Schatzkin, M.D. et al., "Alcohol Consumption and Breast Cancer in the Epidemiologic Follow-Up Study of the First National Health and Nutrition Examination Survey," *The New England Journal of Medicine* 316 (1987): 1169–73; Christine M. Friedenreich et al., "A Cohort Study of Alcohol Consumption and Risk of Breast Cancer," *American Journal of Epidemiology* 137 (1993): 512–20; Stephanie A. Smith-Warner et al., "Alcohol and Breast Cancer in Women: A Pooled Analysis of Cohort Studies," *Journal of the American Medical Association* 279 (1998): 535–40.

2. Mario Frezza, M.D., "High Blood Alcohol Levels in Women," *The New England Journal of Medicine* 322 (1990): 95–99; Ben Morgan Jones and Marilyn K. Jones, "Male and Female Intoxication Levels for Three Alcohol Doses or Do Women Really Get Higher Than Men?" *Alcohol Technical Reports* 5 (1976): 11–14.

3. Ibid., Frezza.

4. Ibid.; Carlo DiPadova et al., "Effects of Fasting and Chronic Alcohol Consumption on the First-Pass Metabolism of Ethanol," *Gastroenterology* 92 (1987): 1170–71.

5. Elizabeth M. Smith, C. Robert Cloninger, M.D., and Susan Bradford, "Predictors of Mortality in Alcoholic Women: A Prospective Follow-Up Study," *Alcoholism: Clinical and Experimental Research* 7 (1983): 237–43.

6. N. Krasner, M.D. et al., "Changing Pattern of Alcoholic Liver Disease in Great Britain: Relation to Sex and Signs of Autoimmunity," *British Medical Journal* 1 (1977): 1499.

7. Robin Jacobson, M.D., "The Contributions of Sex and Drinking History to the CT Brain Scan Changes in Alcoholics," *Psychological Medicine* 16 (1986): 547–59.

8. Clare Acker, "Performance of Female Alcoholics on Neuropsychological Testing," *Alcohol and Alcoholism* 20 (1985): 379–86; Clare Acker, "Neuropsychological Deficits in Alcoholics: The Relative Contributions of Gender and Drinking History," *British Journal of Addiction* 81 (1986): 395–403; see also Judith A. Silberstein and Oscar A. Parsons, "Neuropsychological Impairment in Female Alcoholics: Replication and Extension," *Journal of Abnormal Psychology* 90 (1981): 179–82.

9. See note 7, chap. 17, page 556.

10. Alvaro Urbano-Márquez, M.D. et al., "The Greater Risk of Alcoholic Cardiomyopathy and Myopathy in Women Compared

with Men," *Journal of the American Medical Association* 274 (1995): 149–54.

11. Mary Jane Ashley, M.D. et al., "Morbidity in Alcoholics: Evidence for Accelerated Development of Physical Disease in Women," *Archives of Internal Medicine* 137 (1977): 883–87.

12. Sheila B. Blume, M.D., "Women and Alcohol: A Review," *Journal of the American Medical Association* 256 (1986): 1467.

13. Ibid., 1469.

14. See note 7, chap. 17, page 554.

15. Many alcoholic women have a history of abusing tranquilizers, sedatives, and amphetamines. See note 12, chap. 17, page 1469.

16. Avram Goldstein, M.D., *Addiction: From Biology to Drug Policy* (New York: W. H. Freeman, 1994), 124.

17. Ibid., 4, 128.

**CHAPTER 20: SARAH BETH**

1. This quote, I understand, was paraphrased from *A New Pair of Glasses* (Irvine, California: New-Look Publishing, 1984) by Chuck "C."

**CHAPTER 21: DON'T GET STRESSED OUT IN THE DARK LISTENING TO SLOW MUSIC**

1. Jules H. Masserman and K. S. Yum, "An Analysis of the Influence of Alcohol on Experimental Neuroses in Cats," *Psychosomatic Medicine* 8 (1946): 36–52.

2. Albert Casey, "The Effect of Stress on the Consumption of Alcohol and Reserpine," *Quarterly Journal of Studies on Alcoholism* 21 (1960): 208–16.

3. Irving Geller, "Ethanol Preference in the Rat as a Function of Photoperiod," *Science* 173 (1971): 456–59.

4. Paul J. Bach and James M. Schaefer, "The Tempo of Country Music and the Rate of Drinking in Bars," *Journal of Studies on Alcohol* 40 (1979): 1058–59.

**CHAPTER 22: GOD CREATED ALCOHOL SO THE IRISH WOULDN'T CONQUER THE WORLD—and the Chinese Would**

1. See note 6, chap. 11, page 379.

2. Ibid., 62.

3. J. Westermeyer, "Cross-Cultural Studies on Alcoholism," in *Alcoholism: Biomedical and Genetic Aspects,* edited by H. Werner Goedde and Dharam P. Agarwal (New York: Pergamon Press, 1989), 307.

4. Yildirim B. Dogan, M.D., "Turkey: Drinking Behaviour in a Changing Society," *British Journal of Addiction* 77 (1982): 209–10.

5. Robert K. Thomas, "The History of North American Indian Alcohol Use as a Community-Based Phenomenon," *Journal of Studies on Alcohol* Suppl. 9 (1981): 29–39.

6. See note 3, chap. 22, page 306.

7. Ole-Jørgen Skog, "The Collectivity of Drinking Cultures: A Theory of the Distribution of Alcohol Consumption," *British Journal of Addiction* 80 (1985): 83–99.

8. See Donald W. Goodwin, M.D., "The Alcoholism of F. Scott Fitzgerald," *Journal of the American Medical Association* 212 (1970): 86–90.

9. Sharon C. Wilsnack and Richard W. Wilsnack, "Drinking and Problem Drinking in US Women: Patterns and Recent Trends," in *Recent Developments in Alcoholism, Volume 12: Alcoholism and Women,* edited by Marc Galanter (New York: Plenum Press, 1995), 39, 46; Richard W. Wilsnack, Sharon C. Wilsnack, and Albert D. Klassen, "Women's Drinking and Drinking Problems: Patterns from a 1981 National Survey," *American Journal of Public Health* 74 (1984): 1233–36.

10. Jonathan Chick, "Epidemiology of Alcohol Use and Its Hazards," *British Medical Bulletin* 38 (1982): 4–5.

11. Eric Single, "Public Drinking," in *Recent Developments in Alcoholism, Volume 11: Ten Years of Progress,* edited by Marc Galanter (New York: Plenum Press, 1993), 143–51.

12. Raul Caetano, "Acculturation and Drinking Patterns Among U.S. Hispanics," *British Journal of Addiction* 82 (1987): 796.

13. Walter B. Clark and Michie Hesselbrock, "A Comparative Analysis of U.S. and Japanese Drinking Patterns," in *Cultural Influences and Drinking Patterns: A Focus on Hispanic and Japanese Populations,* edited by Leland H. Towle and Thomas C. Harford. Research Monograph No. 19. DHHS Pub. No. (ADM) 88–1563. (Washington, D.C.: GPO, 1988), 79–98.

14. Harry H. L. Kitano et al., "Alcohol Consumption of Japanese in Japan, Hawaii, and California," in *Cultural Influences and Drink-*

*ing Patterns: A Focus on Hispanic and Japanese Populations,* edited by Leland H. Towle and Thomas C. Harford. Research Monograph No. 19. DHHS Pub. No. (ADM) 88–1563. (Washington, D.C.: GPO, 1988), 104.

15. See note 13, chap. 22, page 97.

16. Joe Yamamoto et al., "Alcohol Abuse Among Koreans and Taiwanese," in *Cultural Influences and Drinking Patterns: A Focus on Hispanic and Japanese Populations,* edited by Leland H. Towle and Thomas C. Harford. Research Monograph No. 19. DHHS Pub. No. (ADM) 88–1563. (Washington, D.C.: GPO, 1988), 135–36.

17. Chung Kyoon Lee, "Alcoholism in Korea," chap. 14 in *Alcoholism in North America, Europe, and Asia,* edited by John E. Helzer, M.D., and Glorisa J. Canino (New York: Oxford University Press, 1992), 247, 255.

## CHAPTER 25: IT'S ALL IN YOUR HEAD

1. Carlton K. Erickson, professor and head of the Addiction Science Research and Education Center, College of Pharmacology, University of Texas at Austin, "Understanding Addictive Disorders: Brain, Behavior, and Treatment," oral presentation at a seminar for health professionals (Atlanta, 1995).

2. See note 16, chap. 17, pages 53–54. It's called the medial forebrain bundle.

3. See note 1, chap. 25.

4. This is the mesolimbic circuit, which extends from the ventral tegmental area to the nucleus accumbens and into the frontal cortex. See note 16, chap. 17, pages 54–55, and David A. Gorelick, "Pharmacological Treatment," in *Recent Developments in Alcoholism, Volume 11: Ten Years of Progress,* edited by Marc Galanter (New York: Plenum Press, 1993), 420–21.

5. "Genetic and Other Risk Factors for Alcoholism," chap. 3 in the Eighth Special Report to the U.S. Congress on Alcohol and Health, U.S. Department of Health and Human Services (NIAAA). (Washington, D.C.: U.S. Government Printing Office, 1993), 8.

6. Samuel H. Barondes, "Thinking About Prozac," *Science* 263 (1994): 1102–03.

7. J. M. Murphy et al., "Contents of Monoamines in Forebrain Regions of Alcohol-Preferring (P) and -Nonpreferring (NP) Lines of

Rats," *Pharmacology, Biochemistry, and Behavior* 26 (1987): 389–92. Nerve transmission in the serotonin receptors is also reduced. F. C. Zhou et al., "Serotonergic Neurons in Alcohol Preferring Rats," *Alcohol* 11 (1994): 397–403. Animals with the highest serotonin activity have the lowest alcohol intake. See note 4, chap. 25, David A. Gorelick, 419.

8. K. Yoshimoto et al., "Alcohol Stimulates the Release of Dopamine and Serotonin in the Nucleus Accumbens," *Alcohol* 9 (1991): 17–22.

9. W. J. McBride et al., "Serotonin, Dopamine and GABA Involvement in Alcohol Drinking of Selectively Bred Rats," *Alcohol* 7 (1990): 199–205. Substances that enhance natural actions are called "agonists."

10. Raye Z. Litten and John P. Allen, "Reducing the Desire to Drink: Pharmacology and Neurobiology," in *Recent Developments in Alcoholism, Volume 11: Ten Years of Progress,* edited by Marc Galanter (New York: Plenum Press, 1993), 326–27.

11. Ewa Jankowska, Andrzej Bidzinski, and Wojciech Kostowski, "Alcohol Drinking in Rats Treated With 5,7-Dihydroxytryptamine: Effect of 8-OH-DPAT and Tropisetron (ICS 205–930)," *Alcohol* 11 (1994), 283.

12. Some prescription drugs selectively block the serotonin transponder, inhibiting the removal or uptake of serotonin from the synapse and enhancing its effect. These are known as "selective serotonin reuptake inhibitors" (SSRIs) and include Prozac and its progeny. See note 6, chap. 25. Although these SSRIs have been effective in treating depression, their impact on alcohol consumption appears to be negligible.

13. See note 7, chap. 25, F.C. Zhou et al.

14. See note 16, chap. 17, page 44.

15. James C. Ballenger, M.D. et al., "Alcohol and Central Serotonin Metabolism in Man," *Archives of General Psychiatry* 36 (1979): 224–27.

16. See note 24, chap. 13, page 83.

17. For excellent reviews of this complex area, see Howard Cappell and Janet Greeley, "Alcohol and Tension Reduction: An Update on Research and Theory," in *Psychological Theories of Drinking and Alcoholism,* edited by Howard T. Blane and Kenneth E. Leonard (New York: Guilford Press, 1987), 15–54, and

L. A. Pohorecky, "Interaction of Ethanol and Stress: Research With Experimental Animals—An Update," *Alcohol and Alcoholism* 25 (1990): 263–76.

18. Christoph H. Wilde and Wolfgang H. Vogel, "Influence of the 5-HT1A Receptor Agonist Ipsapirone on Voluntary Alcohol Intake in Rats," *Alcohol* 11 (1994): 411–15; D. M. Collins and R. D. Myers, "Buspirone Attenuates Volitional Alcohol Intake in the Chronically Drinking Monkey," *Alcohol* 4 (1987): 49–56.

19. See note 6, chap. 11, pages 79–80. However, notice that pre-existing anxiety, for some, does appear to lead to excessive alcohol consumption. For example, people with panic disorder are four times more likely to be addicted. Animal tests have also shown that monkeys raised by peers, rather than by their mothers, are predisposed to increased fear-related behavior and excessive alcohol consumption. Separating mother-reared monkeys from their moms creates major stress for the young and elevates their drinking to almost the same level. J. D. Higley et al., "Nonhuman Primate Model of Alcohol Abuse: Effects of Early Experience, Personality, and Stress on Alcohol Consumption," *Proceedings of the National Academy of Sciences* 88 (1991): 7261–65. And, finally, medical students whose reaction to stress was one of anxiety subsequently were much more likely to abuse alcohol. Richard D. Moore, M.D., Lucy Mead, and Thomas A. Pearson, M.D., "Youthful Precursors of Alcohol Abuse in Physicians," *American Journal of Medicine* 88 (1990): 332–36.

20. Marc A. Schuckit, M.D., "Genetic and Clinical Implications of Alcoholism and Affective Disorder," *American Journal of Psychiatry* 143 (1986): 140–47.

21. Sandra A. Brown, Michael Irwin, M.D., and Marc A. Schuckit, M.D., "Changes in Depression Among Abstinent Alcoholics," *Journal of Studies on Alcohol* 49 (1988): 412–17 and "Changes in Anxiety among Abstinent Male Alcoholics," *Journal of Studies on Alcohol* 52 (1991): 55–61.

22. Marc A. Schuckit, M.D., Michael Irwin, M.D., and Sandra A. Brown, "The History of Anxiety Symptoms among 171 Primary Alcoholics," *Journal of Studies on Alcohol* 51 (1990): 34–41.

23. Shepard Siegel, "Alcohol and Opiate Dependence: Re-evaluation of the Victorian Perspective," in *Research Advances in*

*Alcohol and Drug Problems,* Volume 9, edited by Howard D. Cappell et al. (New York: Plenum Press, 1986), 279–314.

24. Donald W. Goodwin, M.D., *Alcoholism: The Facts,* 2d ed. (New York: Oxford University Press, 1994), 133–34.

25. Virginia E. Davis and Michael J. Walsh, "Alcohol, Amines, and Alkaloids: A Possible Biochemical Basis for Alcohol Addiction," *Science* 167 (1970): 1005.

26. See note 1, chap. 25.

27. "Neurobehavioral Aspects of Alcohol Consumption," chap. 5 in the Eighth Special Report to the U.S. Congress on Alcohol and Health. U.S. Department of Health and Human Services (NIAAA). (Washington, D.C.: U.S. Government Printing Office, 1993), 8.

28. Stephanie S. O'Malley et al., "Naltrexone and Coping Skills Therapy for Alcohol Dependence: A Controlled Study," *Archives of General Psychiatry* 49 (1992): 883–84.

29. Joseph R. Volpicelli, M.D. et al., "Naltrexone in the Treatment of Alcohol Dependence," *Archives of General Psychiatry* 49 (1992): 876.

30. Indeed, six months after naltrexone treatment is discontinued, patients have no better drinking outcome than if they'd been given a placebo. Stephen S. O'Malley et al., "Six-Month Follow-Up of Naltrexone and Psychotherapy for Alcohol Dependence," *Archives of General Psychiatry* 53 (1996): 217–24.

31. There are other neurotransmitters and receptor subtypes involved in the biochemistry of alcohol that are not discussed in the text. One of these is norepinephrine. Another is glutamate, which is a major excitatory transmitter in the brain, one of whose receptors—the NMDA receptor—plays a role in memory. Chronic alcohol use suppresses NMDA receptor function. In addition, these receptors may become hyperactive during alcohol withdrawal, contributing to the convulsions suffered by some people. "Actions of Alcohol on the Brain," chap. 4 in the Eighth Special Report to the U.S. Congress on Alcohol and Health. U.S. Department of Health and Human Services (NIAAA). (Washington, D.C.: U.S. Government Printing Office, 1993), 9, 14, 16–17; Enrico Sanna and R. Adron Harris, "Neuronal Ion Channels," in *Recent Developments in Alcoholism, Volume 11: Ten Years of Progress,*

edited by Marc Galanter (New York: Plenum Press, 1993), 173–74.

## CHAPTER 27: WHERE BLINDNESS LEADS

1. See note 6, chap. 11, page 1.

2. All outpatients at the medical clinic of a private teaching hospital were screened with a questionnaire designed to identify alcoholics, and 20.3 percent of the population tested positive. Michele G. Cyr, M.D., and Steven A. Wartman, M.D., "The Effectiveness of Routine Screening Questions in the Detection of Alcoholism," *Journal of the American Medical Association* 259 (1988): 51–54. Similar test results were found at a family practice center with a 19.1 percent rate. A. Lane Leckman, M.D., Berthold E. Umland, M.D., and Maggie Blay, "Prevalence of Alcoholism in a Family Practice Center," *The Journal of Family Practice* 18 (1984): 867–70.

3. Kevin M. Sherin, M.D. et al., "Screening for Alcoholism in a Community Hospital," *The Journal of Family Practice* 15 (1982): 1091–95.

4. See note 6, chapter 11, page 126. Self-reported alcohol consumption accounts for less than 50 percent of sales. Perry F. Smith, M.D. et al., "A Comparison of Alcohol Sales Data with Survey Data on Self-Reported Alcohol Use in 21 States," *American Journal of Public Health* 80 (1990): 309–12.

5. R. E. Popham and W. Schmidt, "Words and Deeds: The Validity of Self-Report Data on Alcohol Consumption," *Journal of Studies on Alcohol* 42 (1981): 356.

6. See note 6, chap. 11, page 181.

7. See note 22, chap. 25.

8. See note 6, chap. 11, page 206.

9. Ibid., 208.

10. Rob Roy MacGregor, M.D., "Alcohol and Immune Defense," *Journal of the American Medical Association* 256 (1986): 1474–78.

11. Wolfgang Schmidt and Jan de Lint, "Causes of Death of Alcoholics," *Quarterly Journal of Studies on Alcoholism* 33 (1972): 174. The true multiples in a chronic alcoholic population are likely much larger. In this Toronto study, for example, a substantial number of pneumonia deaths were simply attributed to "alcoholism." Ibid., 178.

12. Jo Hofmann, M.D. et al., "The Prevalence of Drug-Resistant *Streptococcus Pneumoniae* in Atlanta," *The New England Journal of Medicine* 333 (1995): 481–86.

13. Alexander Tomasz, "Special Report: Multiple-Antibiotic-Resistant Pathogenic Bacteria, A Report on the Rockefeller University Workshop," *The New England Journal of Medicine* 330 (1994): 1247–51.

14. See note 12, chap. 27, page 483.

15. Alexander Tomasz, "The Pneumococcus at the Gates," *The New England Journal of Medicine* 333 (1995): 514.

16. Ibid., 515.

17. Thomas R. Frieden, M.D. et al., "The Emergence of Drug-Resistant Tuberculosis in New York City," *The New England Journal of Medicine* 328 (1993): 521–26.

18. Marian Goble, M.D. et al., "Treatment of 171 Patients with Pulmonary Tuberculosis Resistant to Isoniazid and Rifampin," *The New England Journal of Medicine* 328 (1993): 527–32.

19. Ibid., 531.

20. Susan E. Kline, M.D., Linda L. Hedemark, M.D., and Scott F. Davies, M.D., "Outbreak of Tuberculosis Among Regular Patrons of a Neighborhood Bar," *The New England Journal of Medicine* 333 (1995): 222–27.

21. See note 2, chap. 11, page 109.

22. H. Bergman et al., "Computed Tomography of the Brain and Neuropsychological Assessment of Male Alcoholic Patients and a Random Sample from the General Male Population," Alcohol and Brain Research: Proceedings of the second Magnus Huss Symposium held in Stockholm, 5–8 September 1979, edited by Carl-Magnus Ideström, *Acta Psychiatrica Scandinavica* 62 (1980): 82.

23. See note 2, chap. 11, page 60.

24. Jaswinder S. Gill et al., "Stroke and Alcohol Consumption," *The New England Journal of Medicine* 315 (1986): 1045.

25. This observed result for women was parenthetically noted in a brief report titled, "Stroke Affecting Young Men After Alcoholic Binges," *British Medical Journal* 291 (1985): 1645, written by J. S. Gill, A. V. Zezulka, and D. G. Beevers.

26. See note 6, chap. 11, page 210.

27. Ibid., 205.

28. Frederick Lemere, M.D., "What Happens to Alcoholics," *American Journal of Psychiatry* 109 (1953): 675. A later study found the mean age of death for chronic alcoholics to be fifty-two years as well. Gerald M. Cross et al., "Alcoholism Treatment: A Ten-Year Follow-Up Study," *Alcoholism: Clinical and Experimental Research* 14 (1990): 171–72.

29. See note 6, chap. 11, page 209; see also, Sidney Pell and C. A. D'Alonzo, M.D., "A Five-Year Mortality Study of Alcoholics," *Journal of Occupational Medicine* 15 (1973): 120–25.

30. Richard D. Hurt, M.D. et al., "Mortality Following Inpatient Addictions Treatment: Role of Tobacco Use in a Community-Based Cohort," *Journal of the American Medical Association* 275 (1996): 1097–1103.

31. Richard D. Hurt, M.D. et al., "Nicotine Dependence Treatment During Inpatient Treatment for Other Addictions: A Prospective Intervention Trial," *Alcoholism: Clinical and Experimental Research* 18 (1994): 867–72.

## CHAPTER 28: WHAT CAN I DO?

1. Cf. cystic fibrosis and muscular dystrophy, where gene therapy is now occurring, but scientists are finding the process extremely complex even after identifying the responsible defective genes. See note 1, chap. 25.

2. David W. Foy, L. Bruce Nunn, and Robert G. Rychtarik, "Broad-Spectrum Behavioral Treatment for Chronic Alcoholics: Effects of Training Controlled Drinking Skills," *Journal of Consulting and Clinical Psychology* 52 (1984): 218–30.

3. Robert G. Rychtarik et al., "Five-Six-Year Follow-Up of Broad-Spectrum Behavioral Treatment for Alcoholism: Effects of Training Controlled Drinking Skills," *Journal of Consulting and Clinical Psychology* 55 (1987): 106–08.

4. See note 6, chap. 11, page 237.

5. By age forty-eight, 40 percent of Dr. Vaillant's college sample had seen psychiatrists. Ibid., 311. "Once recovered, several of the College sample saw their psychotherapy as having retarded recognition of their alcoholism." Ibid., 359.

6. Martha Sanchez-Craig, Karen Spivak, and Rafaela Davila,

"Superior Outcome of Females over Males After Brief Treatment for the Reduction of Heavy Drinking: Replication and Report of Therapist Effects," *British Journal of Addiction* 86 (1991): 873, 875.

7. Chad D. Emrick, "A Review of Psychologically Oriented Treatment of Alcoholism: II. The Relative Effectiveness of Different Treatment Approaches and the Effectiveness of Treatment versus No Treatment," *Journal of Studies on Alcohol* 36 (1975): 97–98.

8. Helen M. Pettinati et al., "The Natural History of Alcoholism over Four Years After Treatment," *Journal of Studies on Alcohol* 43 (1982): 205. Note also the success of employer-mandated treatment reported by Diana Chapman Walsh et al., "A Randomized Trial of Treatment Options for Alcohol-Abusing Workers," *New England Journal of Medicine* 325 (1991): 775–82.

9. John J. Sheehan, Robert J. Wieman, and James E. Bechtel, "Follow-Up of a Twelve-Month Treatment Program for Chronic Alcoholics," *The International Journal of the Addictions* 16 (1981): 233–41.

10. John F. C. McLachlan and Rodeen L. Stein, "Evaluation of a Day Clinic for Alcoholics: Six-Month Outcomes," *Journal of Studies on Alcohol* 43 (1982): 261–72.

11. Richard Longabaugh et al., "Cost Effectiveness of Alcoholism Treatment in Partial v. Inpatient Settings," *Journal of Studies on Alcohol* 44 (1983): 1049–71.

12. Edgar P. Nace, "Inpatient Treatment," *Recent Developments in Alcoholism, Volume 11: Ten Years of Progress,* edited by Marc Galanter (New York: Plenum Press, 1993), 435.

13. See note 13, chap. 13, page 285. Many insurance carriers attempt to forcibly assign *everyone* to outpatient care following detoxification, relying on studies that show comparable success rates between randomly assigned inpatients and outpatients. That is regrettable, since these studies often involve patients who agree to random assignment because they don't need inpatient care. Donald W. Wesson, M.D., and Walter Ling, M.D., "Addiction Medicine," *Journal of the American Medical Association* 275 (1996): 1792–93.

14. See note 24, chap. 13, page 61.

15. John and Pat O'Neill, *Concerned Intervention: When Your Loved One Won't Quit Alcohol or Drugs* (Oakland: New Harbinger Publications, 1993).

16. See note 28, chap. 27, Gerald M. Cross et al., pages 169–73.

17. See note 24, chap. 13, pages 45–46, citing a 1986 survey by the World Services Office of AA.

18. See note 28, chap. 27, Gerald M. Cross et al., page 172.

19. Klaus Mäkelä, "Social and Cultural Preconditions of Alcoholics Anonymous (AA) and Factors Associated with the Strength of AA," *British Journal of Addiction* 86 (1991): 1405–13.

20. See note 5, chap. 15, page 526.

21. With many thanks to the famous physicist Richard P. Feynman, in *"Surely You're Joking, Mr. Feynman!"* (New York: Bantam Books, 1989) and his discussion about hypnotism on page 55. In this regard, alcohol's cumulative biochemical effect on the brain has the same power as hypnotic suggestion.

## CHAPTER 29: THINKING PERSON'S TEST

1. Frequency and quantity questions are of doubtful validity in screening for addiction, and they are not used here. Michele G. Cyr, M.D., and Steven A. Wartman, M.D., "The Effectiveness of Routine Screening Questions in the Detection of Alcoholism," *Journal of the American Medical Association* 259 (1988): 51–54. The exception being question number seven, which is really an indicator of state of mind and was suggested in an enlightening book by Caroline Knapp, *Drinking: A Love Story* (New York: Dial Press, 1996), 52.